TINY ACTIONS
BIG RESULTS

*How a Few Minutes a Day Can Help You
Get and Keep Your Life Together*

JESSICA RILEY BEEBE

To all those who have encouraged me. Thank you!

Table of Contents

Introduction

About 10 years ago I was watching a television interview with Toni Braxton's sisters and one of them said "Girl! Get your LIFE together!" I felt like she was speaking directly to me. I was newly married, teaching full time, had recently bought a house, was coaching Varsity tennis and felt like I just couldn't keep up with things. I couldn't "get my life together." My house seemed messy, teaching felt difficult, coaching was exhausting, and making dinner felt like climbing Mt Everest. I felt disorganized despite watching cleaning videos and decluttering all the time. Getting dinner on the table felt like my biggest struggle every day even though it was just one of many. Life was just overwhelming. And yet, on the outside, things appeared great. I had a great job, a great husband, a new home, and a great coaching job. Life SHOULD have been easy but it was far from it.

Looking back, I realized I was trying to achieve a lot of goals…personal, professional, health, financial, etc. I would make a New Year's Resolution (like I did every year since turning 12) and when I didn't achieve everything by March, I would consider myself a failure and go right back to whatever habits or lifestyle I had been living. (I am not alone, most people drop their resolutions by February, so I was a champ to make it to March!) But, I was disappointed. I hadn't expected it to be easy but I also didn't expect it to be impossible. I also never hit "rock bottom" like all the books you read and movies you watch, so I figured that I should just be grateful for what I had and get over it. But something inside me kept gnawing at me. ALL the goal gurus would tell you to:

1. Start with a big goal
2. Break it into tiny steps
3. Then just achieve all the little tiny steps until you reach your goal.

It seemed reasonable enough but I could never seem to get over the hump of not seeming to make any progress. There had to be a better way!

In my free time, I started reading books, articles, testimonials, and anything motivational. I experimented with diets, workouts, financial programs, etc. I researched online. I tried hundreds of different methods, and when I failed, I became curious instead of becoming angry or frustrated. All of this knowledge led me to where I am today. This mini book is a compilation of all my research and trial and error. I have broken this book into 4 sections.

1. Chapter 1 Mind the Gap (why I failed at goals and you probably are failing too)

2. Chapter 2 Crack the Code (how I cracked the code of goal setting and achievement)

3. Chapters 3-6 (all the specific little tips that I have used to get where I am today-Money/Health/Work/School/Home)

4. Chapter 7 Fall back (Failure)

5. Chapter 8 Charge Ahead (Bursts)

6. Chapter 9 Day in the Life

7. Chapter 10 What now? (Where do I go from here)

8. Appendix-forms, notes, suggestions, etc. for further development

Chapter 1
Mind the Gap

Start where you are… ***"Mind the Gap"***

Recognize where you are on the journey of a specific goal. This is more important than the goal or the steps you are taking to achieve that specific goal.

In London, when you ride the underground subway, there is a loudspeaker that tells you to *"mind the gap."* He is telling you to watch out for the gap between the platform and the train. This is good advice for the subway and also for life. In this chapter, I talk about what I think goal setters get wrong and how I have learned to fix it. Too many people do not *"mind the gap"* between where they currently are and where they want to be. This creates problems and most people give up on their goals easily.

When we were younger, a lot of our goals were already mapped out for us. In the USA, a person completes Kindergarten through 12th grade and then is given a high school diploma. At each grade you review some content and learn a little more. Yes, some years are stressful, but it is a nice system that helps you achieve the goal of graduation. For the most part, there isn't much of a gap. The years lead into each other and your prize is a diploma at the end.

It is similar in sports. Take baseball as an example. You play Tball, then little league and then Jr Varsity and then Varsity. A natural progression. Again, no gap.

If there is a gap, adults are there to help you to *"mind the gap"* between where you are and where you want to be. They show you steps to take in order to achieve your goals.

However, when we get to be adults, we have a ton of stuff thrown at us and pretty soon we are barely hanging on or we are successful in one area of life and the other areas are a hot mess.

So what do we do? Mind the gap and remember that it is ALWAYS there and it is sometimes bigger than other times. Let me give you an example of a fitness gap.

When I was in the best shape of my life, I was working out for about 45 minutes a day (20 walk/25 elliptical) lifting (small weights for arms) 6 days a week. I was also teaching all day, living alone, and frankly, not eating much because I lived alone and it was my first big jump into adulthood…i.e. My job didn't pay much. Fortunately or unfortunately, I always seem to hold that standard in my head as the "if I can't get back to that weight/fitness level, then I am out of shape." Did I mention I was 26 yrs. old at the time? So for years I did everything I could to get back to that weight/level. What I forgot to take into account was the fact that my lifestyle had changed, my job had changed, my gym had changed, and I started having health problems (certain medications made me gain weight). I would try to diet and exercise to get back there and after a few weeks, it was too hard, so I gave up. (Now I can see that the gap from where I was to where I wanted to be which was as big as the Grand Canyon)

I did this EVERY New Year's Eve with every new goal.

I wanted to save money.

I wanted to get into shape.

I wanted to spend more time with people I cared about.

I wanted to be less stressed.

I wanted a clean house.

I wanted to excel at my job.

After years of goal setting and being frustrated, I figured there had to be a better way. And now, I think I have found it.

First of all, you have to "mind the gap" between where you currently are and where you want to be. You have to get super honest about where you are and then put small little steps in place to help you get there. This may sound repetitive for some but I can't tell you how many times I see people charge ahead with a goal, only to give up 1, 2, 3 months later because it was too hard. Of course it was too hard! You were so far away from your target that of course you failed.

So, this book is all the tiny little steps I have taken to shrink the gap. I still have the goals. I have just learned and practiced these tiny actions, repeatedly, and the gaps disappeared or lessened to the point where I could see the end.

Beware of other people (They ARE the gap)

We have a tendency to look out into the world and see the progress of others. However, we never saw what they did "in the gap." We only see what they have now and we want it for ourselves. Think of Tom Brady and multiple Super Bowl Rings. He has put small effective habits into place for YEARS (DECADES) and that is why if we (or any other football player) wanted to get to where he is, we would have to start closing that gap between where we are and where he currently resides.

Let me give you a more concrete example. I played high school tennis in a small town in Michigan. For over 25 years, my coach took a team to the state finals and had multiple state champions. Our town was not a "typical tennis town" and we would have to compete against very wealthy schools that were frankly very surprised to see us there. So how did we do it? My coach was able to find out what those teams did and then proceed to have us behave just like them in order to close our gap.

When we would play league matches, we would beat the pants off of people. We would easily roll through the Regional tournament and would regularly be ranked as one of the top 10 teams in the state of Michigan. (My coach was inducted to the Hall of Fame twice and he doesn't even really know how to play tennis!)

So what did we do differently than other schools? (I didn't really learn this until I started coaching high school tennis, 15 years later.)

1. We NEVER left practice early (You would be surprised how many kids try to duck out early on a Friday) and every practice was intense. We didn't have "fun" practices. "Fun" was winning matches.

2. We played 5 days a week, all summer long, from the time we were about 8 years old.

3. We took lessons with a Pro on Saturdays (my coach knew he couldn't help us with the game, but he got us to someone who could)

4. We played tournaments that got us ranked with some of the best in the state.

5. We played multiple sports so we didn't burn out on tennis.

6. Our coach was our guidance counselor and so could make sure we had appropriate class loads (not too easy or too hard during tennis season.)

7. We had "two-a-days" just like football for the first week of tryouts those matches set the lineup and my coach could NOT be persuaded by tears, parents, etc…

8. We attended team camps.

9. My coach helped purchase equipment for kids who didn't have the money to play but were great athletes and turned them into great tennis players.

I just assumed that all kids did these things because this was my reality. Boy, was I wrong! Now I realize that all those things set us apart from other teams. No wonder how we beat the pants off people! And then we got to the state tournament and some of us lost. I found out later that those kids who beat us had nutritionists, indoor courts, trainers, etc… It was a whole other level from us and mathematically they should have beaten us.

So that's what I mean by the gap. Are you the kid in used tennis shoes and you are trying to beat Serena Williams? Not going to happen. That may seem like a silly example so I will give you one that hits closer to home.

Are you the person who wants to have a perfect bikini body but you have always been about 20 pounds overweight? I am NOT saying you can't have that body. Instead, I am saying to look at where you are and what you do and what that person does and see how you can close the gap. Victoria Beckham has eaten the SAME food of grilled chicken and vegetables for over 20 years. Candace Cameron has given up sugar, flour, dairy and works out a lot. If these people have a better body than you, you have to look at what they are doing to achieve it and then take stock of what you are doing to achieve yours. (Cookies on Saturdays are FINE…but Victoria and Candace don't eat them)

Once you see the gap, you can decide if you want to do everything in your power to close that gap.

If you want to be Tom Brady, are you willing to do everything he does?

If you want to be the state ranked D1 swimmer, are you willing to get up every morning of your summer vacation, drive an hour away and swim for 2 hours BEFORE your team practice?

If you want to win the wrestling state title in high school, are you willing to spend EVERY Saturday for 10 years on a gym mat?

If you want to win a state bowling title, are you willing to not pick up your golf state medal so that you can get into an RV with your dad and drive two hours to make it in time for another bowling tournament?

If you want to have a bikini body, do you want to devote every single meal and gym experience toward making that happen? Give up sugar, flour, dairy?

And if the answer is yes, AWESOME! Go for it! But if the answer is no…read on

These are high level goals and extreme examples of success. You may be thinking to yourself, "I just want to have my house picked up, have my pants fit, get a raise at work, and keep my sanity. I don't need to be Tom Brady."

If that is you, read on!

Chapter 2
Crack the Code

Are you baby stepping, bursting, maintaining or retreating?

"Get to it!" my grandma always used to say. So let's get to it.

Four books I read that were very influential to my thinking were James Clear's <u>Atomic Habits</u>, Stephen Guise's <u>Mini Habits</u>, BJ Fogg's <u>Tiny Habits</u>, and Charles Duhigg's <u>Power of Habit</u>. These men have provided all the scientific reasoning behind habit forming and why you need to start small. They have tons of research, all the scientific reasoning behind habits, great examples, etc. and they would tell you to break down your goals into tiny little steps and get going!

They were wonderful and yet, I felt as though something was missing. I am not a guy. I do not have a pushup or flossing goal. I was just trying to keep my house and life together. I wanted concrete examples. (Their books were geared towards helping you design your own goal) I wanted specific, DO THIS examples, and I wanted to hear the stories behind them and how they came to doing those tiny little actions. I also wanted to hear more about failure or what to do when it wasn't working.

I turned to the Internet and looked for examples from women. The women I would see on Pinterest and YouTube were moms. I didn't see a ton of single women or childless women. How did these people put their lives together? Were they struggling like me or were their lives perfect?

Through a lot of trial and error and research, I started to craft little tiny things that were working for me. Then, I started to doubt myself because these actions seemed so tiny that they were almost ridiculous. So, I stopped doing them.

What I experienced next was shocking.

I stopped doing the little bit of dishes in the sink and left them and it took me an HOUR to get them done when I finally did them.

I left everything on the bathroom counter and it took me 20 minutes to put everything away and clean everything.

I left the laundry for "next week" and it took me a whole day to get through.

I left things on the dinner table and every day put a little more on it and by the end of the week it took me 10-15 minutes to clean everything off and put it all away in the proper place.

I left my desk at school a mess and the next day it put me in a bad mood.

I didn't take things with me from room to room and it seemed like nothing ever got put away!

So IT ALL MATTERED! I couldn't believe it! I started to believe that I had stumbled upon something amazing, and I needed to keep testing it. Hence, this book.

However, even with all these tiny actions, something still felt off. I had days where I was achieving way more (bursts) and days where I wasn't doing much of anything. So, what was up with that? And what about when I would stop doing something and backslide on my goals or progress? It was this exact area that made me have to dig deeper. There had to be an explanation and I HAD to find a way around these occurrences. It came to me on my treadmill one day.

I think we are always in 3 stages of something that we are experiencing (4 if you count retreating but we are going to focus on the first 3 for now)

1. Survive and Advance (maintenance)

2. Tiny steps forward

3. Bursts forward

4. Retreating but we are trying to stay away from that for now.

For example, let's take the goal of weight loss. We see a magazine article or diet book that promises "Lose 30 pounds in 30 days" and we get excited. We want to lose 30 pounds! And we can do it in 30 days-YES! So we start the diet, start working out and may even lose a couple pounds that first week. Then, we don't lose weight in week 2 and we get frustrated. We keep trying the program and maybe lose 1-2 pounds in week 3 but then week 4 creeps up and we have lost nothing. We feel like a failure. We only lost a total of 4 pounds-we were supposed to lose THIRTY! So we give up, go to the grocery store, buy an entire bag of cookies and eat them all before we even get out of the parking lot. That's just me? Oh ok (it's ok-I know you have done it too and just don't want to admit it) Then we retreat back into our old habits and ways until we try again to lose the weight.

We were in burst mode for 30 days and when our results were not as promised, we think we have failed.

In my opinion, every goal should be attacked in 3 ways (tiny steps, bursts forward, maintenance) and we should avoid #4 (retreating) at all costs. But that is not how we currently do things. We "go burst or go home."

What if we recognized the bursts for what they were and when they were over, went back to tiny steps and maintenance? Could it really be that simple? So I started looking at some of the goals I was trying to achieve and broke my actions into "tiny steps, maintenance, and bursts."

If it pertained to housekeeping…

Did I want to spend all day cleaning my house? If I did, AWESOME! (Bursting)

Did I want to just do a few minutes a day so that my weekends were free? (Babystepping)

Did I want to do even less and just maintain the house like it is? Already had a few systems in place that seemed to work. (Maintaining)

If it pertained to money…

Did I want to put my entire tax refund or Birthday money into savings? (Bursting)

Did I want to save $1.00 a day? (Babystepping)

Did I want to keep doing what I was currently doing-save a little, spend most? (Maintaining)

If it pertained to getting healthier

Did I want to go on a strict diet/exercise plan? (Bursting)

Did I want to add a banana and a 10 min walk to my day (Babystepping)

Did want to keep doing what I was currently doing…eat ok and exercise sometimes (Maintaining)

If it pertains to school (student version)

Do you want to banish the television from the house and spend every night studying? (Bursting)

Do you want to reread your notes after dinner and research about a topic on the internet for 10 min? (Babystepping)

Do you want to keep doing what you are currently doing-sleeping through class and cramming info for the test? (Maintaining)

If it pertained to work

Did I want to show up early every day, stay late every night, work through my lunch? (Bursting)

Did I want to show up a little early, to work on a new project, before everyone gets in the office? (Babystepping)

Did I want to keep doing what I was currently doing by showing up early but when work was over, leave everything and run out the door? (Maintaining)

I saw that I could either maintain and keep getting what I was getting or I could add in a few baby steps to a few areas and see what changed. Every once in a while, I would have a burst and instead of counting that as my new level, I would simply return to the baby stepping when the burst was over.

It started working. I didn't feel like I was failing when I couldn't "burst" all the time. And I was making progress! Slowly but surely! My bank account was growing, my pants were getting looser, and my house was cleaner. I felt less stressed and more accomplished! It was amazing.

The choice is yours. You get to decide what to focus on. You get to decide if you are going to maintain, baby step forward or burst toward a goal. This book is mostly about the tiny actions-the next book will be more about the bursts.

Read on to see the very specific and very tiny actions I have been putting into place and how you can incorporate them into your own life.

Chapter 3
Money

I am starting with money because it is the easiest for me and I think I have always been relatively good at saving. It is also super concrete. Numbers don't lie. Each section will have all the tips listed for quick reference and then a story or explanation farther down that you can skip to if you are intrigued or confused.

1. Save $1.00 a day
2. Save your change
3. Savings accounts for separate expenses
4. Save all year for recurring expenses
5. Have a preset plan for "unexpected money" BEFORE the money hits your account
6. Make it a game/challenge
7. Make do without for a little while
8. No spend challenge
9. Weekly deductions
10. Make the tough choices now
11. If this is hard for you, start with a different one or you are going too fast/too much
12. Use your credit card miles for "rewards for yourself for doing the right thing"
13. Carry cash

14. Have a running tally in your head or purse or wallet
15. Use up what you have
16. Beware of "discounts/sales"
17. Borrow instead of buy
18. Find a second way to make money but don't count that as your "income"
19. Roll money over to the next week
20. Always have a cushion (emergency/confidence 100)
21. Cut expenses where it doesn't matter to you
22. Know your "high buying times"
23. Make a plan for giving/tithing
24. Check your accounts regularly (once a week minimum)
25. Visualize what the money you are saving is going toward
26. Sometimes you should piecemeal and sometimes you shouldn't
27. Save for large purchases the minute you make them, start saving again
28. Ask yourself WHY you want the thing
29. Stop worrying about making other people uncomfortable
30. Start yourself and pull others along slowly with you.
31. Decide on Christmas presents early and purchase part of them each week.
32. Buy a gift card every time you go grocery shopping
33. Think about maintenance, not just the initial purchase.
34. Sell stuff online
35. Find a way to make more money at the job you currently have
36. Find a part time job that sells something you want
37. Get out of debt and stay out of debt
38. Invest early
39. Use your raises and bonuses wisely
40. DO NOT spend the money before you have it.

41. Simplify. Simplify. Simplify

42. Buy Quality

43. Learn what works for you

44. Don't use the same system for every part of life

45. Don't discount your own dreams to make the dreams of others come true

46. Can you combine two goals?

47. It can't hurt to ask

48. Stock up on household supplies that can never expire

49. Have a signature wedding/graduation gift that you give to people.

50. Round up.

51. Save up to pay large bills all at once to get a discount.

52. $5.00/$1.00/quarter/dime game

53. Being organized saves money

54. Pay bills/check accounts on Fridays

55. Use a purchase pause (24hr/36hr/48hr)

56. Delay don't deny.

57. Get rid of the "it has to be perfect" mindset

58. Don't compete with friends or family.

1.   Save $1.00 a day

There are 365 days in a year. If you are just starting your savings journey, can you save a dollar a day? If you can't, can you save 50 cents a day? If not, can you save 25 cents a day? How little can you save to the point where it seems ridiculous and totally doable?

So about 2 years ago, I found out that the 2024 Olympics were going to be in Paris, France. I have wanted to go back to Paris for some time now and my husband has always wanted to go to the Olympics so we thought this would be perfect. That day, I started having $7.00 a week deducted from my bank account ($1.00 a day). It doesn't seem like much and we have 6 years to save. So in reality if that is ALL I save, I will only save like 2400ish dollars…definitely not enough to get us to Paris. However, and this is the biggest part, it created momentum. There was a fund in my bank that said Paris Olympics on it. I got an Eiffel Tower Piggy Bank that is on my bedroom dresser. Every time I check my account I see that it rises by a few dollars and I smile. $7.00 in Paris is a Croissant and a cafe au lait. $14.00 is a baguette and a glass of wine. $21.00 is lunch at a restaurant and $28.00 is dinner for 1 night.

I have since increased that amount to $2.00 a day and now I am at $3.00 a day. I took a different job and had to take a pretty sizable pay cut so I have not been able to increase that number for a year or so. However, now that I feel comfortable with my new paycheck, I can increase that to maybe $4.00 a day or $5.00 a day. ALSO DON'T just lump it. Like ($21.00 a week). Add the increments slowly and also leave them as $7.00 a week so that if you have to cut one out, you don't cut out all of it. An example of this is when I felt like my budget was a little too tight, I cut two of my $7.00 a week auto deductions but left one of them.

2.   Save your spare change.

When I was in high school, there was a man on the Oprah Winfrey show that had NEVER spent his spare change for 18 years (he started the minute his wife became pregnant with their son) and he used that to put his son through college (80,000 dollars!) This was his tip.

Every time you pay, pay in cash. Even if something is $2.02…DO NOT GIVE THE CASHIER TWO PENNIES! Instead, pay with $3.00 and take the 98 Cents and put it in a jar. (There are now even credit cards and apps that will do this for online purchases and put it into a retirement account…Acorns is one.)

So I started doing this from the moment that I saw that episode. It was so fun to watch the money pile up in a piggy bank. I am sure that I annoyed Cashiers but I didn't care. And many times I have had them say "do you have a dime with you?" "Nope, I don't. Please give me back the 90 cents."

At first, this annoyed my husband. I would actually yell at him when he would pull change out of his pocket and pay for something. I tried to convince him but he didn't see it. He hadn't seen that Oprah show like I had. He didn't understand. So, I simply did it and didn't bug him. Then when I rolled almost $400.00 worth of change and paid for all the meals on our vacation, he became a believer! Have a very specific fund that the money goes to-something that means a lot to you (car, college, vacation, etc…)

3.   **Savings accounts for separate expenses (Capital one) Auto deduct.**

Almost 13 years ago I was introduced to Capital One (at the time it was ING Orange) and they let you open as many savings accounts as you wanted. So, I opened an account because the boyfriend I had at the time, I thought I would marry him. That didn't end up happening. I was putting away money for a wedding. So, Instead I used that money to go on a trip by myself.

Before that I felt as though I would do what most people do. I had one savings account and one checking account and each time I got paid I would transfer a little to savings if I had not spent it that pay period. Sometimes, I would have money to transfer and sometimes I didn't. But I couldn't really tell where all my money had gone each week. I paid off my credit card every few weeks and I transferred a little bit to savings so I thought I was doing well. But after that one account, I realized I could do things differently. I now have 2 checking accounts, 18 savings accounts and 2 retirement accounts. If this seems ridiculous to you, then scroll on past this tip. However, these are my categories of savings. Personal (had before got married) joint savings with hubby, car payments, car insurance, travel, coaching, oh crap fund, writing, teaching supplies, earrings or new phone, rent and bills, Christmas, tithing/giving, IRA, Personal, Paris 1, Paris 2, Daily.

Now some people would call these 'sinking funds". I call them savings accounts and I have the money transferred each week so that when I need to pay that bill or buy that thing, or go on vacation, the money is there. It's also a visual reminder every time I log in, I can see my goal and see how close I am to them.

4. Save all year for recurring expenses (holidays, birthdays, car insurance)

There are expenses in your life that you know will always occur…Christmas, car insurance, your sister's birthday. These things happen every year. They are not a surprise. Save for them all year.

When I was little, my mom told us about this thing called a Christmas club at the local bank. Kids could open a savings account and deposit a little bit each week or month so they had money when it was Christmas time. We started it in June but my mom gave us $5.00 a week to deposit. As a 12-year-old, having $250.00 at Christmas time felt like being a millionaire! That was probably when I fell in love with saving money. She would also let us spend a little on candy and then deposit the rest so some weeks it was $4.00 instead of $5.00 but still the point was made.

That year I bought something for everyone in my family AND my teacher and still had a little money left over to add to any Christmas money I got from my grandparents. It was awesome! As I got older, I stopped contributing to the Christmas club and every year when Christmas came around I would kick myself that I didn't have that $250.00 or more that I could just spend on presents. Well, I decided last year to start it again and I am super excited to say that I have almost $425.00 for Christmas presents this year. (I started a little late)

5. Have a preset plan for "unexpected money" BEFORE the money hits your account

As a teacher, I don't get a Christmas bonus or any type of bonus at my job. But sometimes my health insurance will only be deducted twice a month on a 3 paycheck month. Or, I might get a birthday check from grandma. Or during the pandemic I was qualified for hazard pay. Or, I was even teaching when the state took money out of our paycheck that they shouldn't have so they gave us our money back. However, this could include tax refunds or any other type of bonus/unexpected money you receive.

Before you receive the money, think logically about what you would like to do with it and what would give you the most pleasure. Let's say it is $100.00. Do you really need another pair of jeans or shoes or could you put that money toward something else? You should not have been counting on this money. This is not money in your budget. I would recommend either paying off some debt with it (not fun but responsible) or putting it toward something that will be meaningful like a trip. Mine right now is going toward the Paris Olympic trip. I don't need it for anything else because I have budgeted appropriately for all the other expenses in my life.

A recent example of this is my rebate for my contact lenses. I had to purchase them but I qualified for a $250.00 rebate. So, when that rebate came, I used it for my weekly gas and groceries and the money I normally had for that went right into savings. The Paris Olympics fund to be exact.

6.   Make it a game/challenge

Pinterest is a great place for this. I have seen ideas to save every time you get a 5 or 10-dollar bill. I saw someone just recently put together 50 envelopes starting with 1 dollar, 2 dollars and up and so when you have that amount you fill that envelope. I don't really use this idea but it seemed fun to me.

I actually get joy from reworking my budget. It's like a game to me. Once I hit a certain amount in the category, I go to work on the next one

7.   Make do without for a little while

Can you go without a latte this week? Just one of them? Can you simply wear the clothes you have for a month and not buy any others? Can you use the decorations you already have this Christmas instead of buying new? Can you stay home this weekend instead of eating out or going out to a movie?

I am not saying to stop your life! I am saying to put it on pause for a second. Maybe you get a latte every day on the way to work. Can you get a smaller one and save the difference? Can you take coffee from home ONE day and save the $6.00? I am not telling you to give up your coffee. I am just asking you to give it up one day. Maybe only 1 day a month instead of a week?

Other examples:

Can you wait a little while before updating to the latest smartphone?

Can you wait for the book to come from the library instead of ordering and buying it?

8.   No spend challenge

There are many of these on the internet. The basic premise behind it is that you don't spend any money for a certain length of time. One day, one week, one month or one year. This is NOT a tiny action. This is a burst. However, the tiny action would be a no spend day.

I have done a 'No spend November" and I plan to do another one this November as well. The first time I did this I saved a ton of money. My rules were that I could spend money on rent/gas/food but nothing else. No clothes, nothing for my house, nothing for school, no presents, nothing. This is DEFINITELY a burst so this needs to be entered with extreme caution. I have included all my notes from "my no spend November" a few years ago in the appendix if you are curious.

However, this is how I paid off my car early. I also saved up money for our house we are buying. It is really amazing how much money "dribbles out" unexpectedly. $20.00 here…$10.00 there...etc.

9.   Weekly deductions

I started this last year. I get paid every 2 weeks. I take my bills and expenses and see what things cost per week (for example my car payment was $200.00 a month so I deducted 50 a week into my car account).

Here is why it is a little thing that works for me. My union dues don't get deducted for July and August so I have 200.00 extra dollars for school shopping. My car is $200 a month times 12 months which is $2400.00 but $50 a week for 52 weeks is $2600 so an extra $200 a year. You can use this money for whatever you want. I save it for car repairs or registration tags.

10.   Make the tough choices now

Saving $5.00 a week for Christmas makes it so I don't have to find money for Christmas presents. Saving retirement money now makes it so I can someday relax

Saving $1.00 a day now makes it so I don't have to "find the money" to go to Paris Olympics in 4 years

These tough choices happen each day and week so that you don't have to make them later.

11.   If this is hard for you, start with a different tiny action or its too much or too fast

I am good at saving money. I like it. It is fun to me. So I started the tiny actions with this category. If money is/has been hard for you, start with a different category.

12.   Use your credit card miles for "rewards for yourself for doing the right thing" or guilty pleasures

A few years ago I got a credit card that gives me "points". When my husband and I got married, we used that credit card to pay for a lot of the wedding/honeymoon expenses and then I used those "points" to buy my outdoor furniture. I bought a pair of sandals during quarantine. I bought my nieces birthday present and a fall candle that way.

This is how I buy novels for my classroom…I enjoy reading so it is also a treat for me as well as stocking my classroom library as a teacher.

ONLY DO THIS IF YOU HAVE SELF CONTROL! I can't stress this enough! I DON'T always have control when it comes to resisting cookies. I DO have control when it comes to pulling out my credit card and paying for things. So, this is a small added bonus to buy some of those 'frivolous things' that I don't really need but would like.

13.   Carry cash/Big bills

It has been proven that people are less likely to buy something when they have to part with their cold hard cash. Swiping a card has just become too easy. So, carry cash and pay with it. It will also give you the spare change I was talking about in tip 2

One of my tips is to carry cash in really big bills. A $100.00 bill is a lot of money to me, always has been, and when I see people with $100.00 bills it amazes me. So, if I am carrying a $100.00 bill vs $5-20's I am less inclined to spend it because it seems special. Also, I won't stop for a $3.00 ice cream if all I have in my wallet is a $100.00 bill so it helps keep my health in check as well!

14.   Have a running tally in your head or purse or wallet

Each week I budget $150.00 for groceries and gasoline. After I buy something on my credit card, I deduct from that $150 in my head. So for example, as of right now, I have $75 left this week (filled up my tank on Friday and bought groceries)

I spend the budgeted money on my credit card and pay it off on Friday of each week

15.   Use up what you have

This one is big (or at least it has been for me). Use up the shampoo/soap that is in your shower. Use all those sample bottles that someone gave you. If you have the stuff for meatloaf in your pantry, make meatloaf. Here is an example from my life this weekend. I wanted to make white chicken chili on Saturday and I had all the ingredients so, I did. I also wanted to order takeout on Sunday. However, I have enough chili for my meal on Sunday night (just kind of nibbled for breakfast and lunch). SO I DID NOT GO BUY TAKEOUT! On the one hand, I told myself "It will only be 10-15 bucks and you have plenty of weekly money left. And then Tip 15 screamed at me YOU HAVE CHILI EAT THAT! YOU WON'T DIE!!!!!!!!!

Now here is a small key. I really want the takeout so I made a plan that I will order it on Friday night. It makes swallowing the chili a little more tolerable and I am saving money.

Another example is my essential oil diffuser. I am running out of candles (I burn them all the time when I get home from work. I love the smell and the ambiance) However, instead of going out shopping and possibly being tempted to buy something else I don't need as well, I am using my diffuser and the smell is lovely.

16. Beware of "discounts/sales" and only buy what you need

This is pretty self-explanatory. I do think you need to keep an eye out. Last night I bought a pair of boots that are normally $100.00 and they were $35 with shipping. To be fair though, I had been looking for 2 months. They were not an impulse buy. Keep a list of things you "really need" so that if a great deal comes along, you can take advantage of it. Notice that I did not add things to my cart for free shipping, I did not buy them in brown also, I did not buy a new pair of jeans or a purse or a sweater. I needed the boots. I bought the boots. End of story.

17. Borrow instead of buy

Last year I was going to a tennis conference and needed a stadium seat (it is a padded chair for bleachers). I was going to be sitting on the bleachers for almost 8 hours and I knew my butt couldn't handle it. The kicker was that I had one of those chairs at my parents' house 2 hours away. I had recently moved into an apartment because we sold our house and my parents were housing some of our stuff until we bought another house. They were only 40 bucks. I could have bought one. But with a little texting, I was able to find a friend that would loan me hers- all I had to do was to drive to her house to get it. Saved me 40 bucks and my rear end.

18.   Find a second way to make money but don't count that as your "income"

In college I worked a summer job and saved most of it because my real job was during the school year. During my first few teaching years, I lived off my salary and then saved my coaching check for trips/savings/etc… If you think this is silly, Jay Leno and Jerry Seinfeld do the same thing. They are both comedians and both had TV shows. I can't remember which they considered their "real job." I think it was being a comedian and then they saved every penny from their TV shows.

19.   Roll money over to the next week

At the end of my first week of budgeting, I had 10 dollars left over. I could have put it into savings but I rolled it over so that the next week I had $160. Then at the end of that week I had $30 left over so I had $180 and I needed all 180 that week. I was so glad it was there. Sometimes your budget is off and you will need more than you thought you did. So, roll the money over to the next week so it's there for you in case you need it.

20.   Always have a cushion (emergency 100)

My husband and I always carry an Emergency 100.00 bill in our wallets. His is behind his license and mine is in a zipper pocket. It HAS to be a 100.00 bill. And it needs to be hidden. This is not money you use to buy dinner with. This is not 'whoops I went over my budget this week" money. This is a flat tire on the side of highway money. This is "crap this place only takes cash" money. This is "my friend is in trouble and needs help" money.

21.   Cut expenses where it doesn't matter to you

So, I love cars. I always have. My grandmother does too and so do my parents. I have a Camaro and a Jeep and a few years ago I had a Cadillac SUV. I am a teacher and so we don't have unlimited funds. I had to make cuts in other areas. At one time I was wearing a $4.00 sweater from a secondhand store. No one knew. I looked nice and professional. I was spending my money on my cars. Now, I have cars that are paid off and I spend a bit more on clothing. Some people love Organic food. Then cut down on what you spend for shampoo and soap. Or perhaps, you love traveling and vacations. Then live in a smaller house. Cut the money where it doesn't matter as much to you so that you have money for the things you care about.

22.   Know your "high buying times" for me it is summer and Christmas time

I love summer (I am a teacher and so I get my summers off.) It's a time of vacation and good food and traveling and parties and barbecues. It is super easy to spend money. Also, because I don't work, I have free time to shop or look online.

My other time is Christmas time. I love presents and cookies and all the things that Christmas brings…secret Santa, gifts for coworkers, etc. Lots of advertisements for things, cute Christmas mugs, etc.

These are my weak points and so I needed to come up with a plan for them. My current plan is to save for Christmas all year round and to have a separate savings account for summer. When I have extra money in the fall, it goes into these two categories.

23.   Make a plan for giving/tithing

My dad always says, what goes around comes around. You don't need to be religious to give back to people. Pick a few organizations or causes and give a little. The person in charge of my local United Way ALWAYS said $1.00 a paycheck makes a difference. It always felt silly to me but she was using the tiny steps. If all 400 employees put in $1.00 a paycheck and 26 pays a year, all of the sudden you have over $10,000! That is REAL MONEY!

Decide what is important to you. I give to Feeding America every month. It is important to me that people have food. I can't do everything but I can do that. So when I give, I try to keep my focus on food for others. Otherwise my bleeding heart would bleed me dry. If you absolutely cannot spare a cent, try volunteering your time or service.

24.   Check your accounts regularly (once a week minimum)

Some people may say that checking your bank accounts that's much is excessive however I think at least once a week is a good small easy way to keep a handle on where your money is going or if there are any issues. For example, I have a friend who gave her son her old iPhone and did not realize that it was still linked to her credit card. Because she only checks her statements once a month he was able to ring up almost $500 in charges for a game and he didn't realize he was doing it and she didn't realize he was doing it. When they called the phone company and called the gaming company there really wasn't anything that could be done because it wasn't fraud. He had made the charges and it was basically lack of paying attention and you can't get your money back for that. So I recommend checking your bank account at least once a week if not more than that. That way you can catch any random charges that should not be there and it gives you a good sense of where you are in your budget or if any unexpected money is coming or going out of your account.

25.   Visualize what the money you are saving is going toward (i.e. every $25.00 is a dinner at a restaurant on vacation)

So when I want to buy some small treat I tend to think about what that could buy for my goals. Like $5.00 is a croissant in Paris. $25.00 is a museum ticket in Paris. $50.00 is dinner in Paris with my husband. So, do I really need a new sweater? Usually I tell myself no because I would rather have those things on vacation. I have enough sweaters.

26. Sometimes you should piecemeal and sometimes you shouldn't

I save a majority of my money from my paycheck. I piecemeal it out to certain categories and let it sit there. However, sometimes if I want something quicker (like a vacation) then I will stop all my little savings and instead push everything into my vacation fund for a few weeks so that I have plenty of money in there. Then I return to the piecemealing.

27. Save for large purchases and the minute you make them, start saving again

Cars. Christmas. Vacay. The minute I walk onto the plane to come home I am already putting away a couple dollars for my next vacation. The minute I sign the papers for a car I am putting away money for my next car and so on and so forth.

I had $1000.00 saved for a new smartphone. They were running a promo and so with trade in and everything, it only cost $780.00. That money is staying in the phone account for the next phone even though that is 3 years away! I'm not going to use it to buy new boots, buy more Christmas presents, etc… Of course, if I get in a jam with a bill or something, I could use it but if you compartmentalize it, now I only need 21 dollars a month for the next 3 years to have my new phone paid for in 3 years.

Same with my car. As soon as I paid it off, I started putting $50 a week toward a NEW car for 4 years from now. In 3 years I will have

$7200 saved for a new car and my current car should still be worth about $5,000 so I will have $12,000 toward my next car which is more than enough!

28. **Ask yourself WHY you want the thing-think Diamond earrings.**

I wanted a pair of diamond stud earrings. I wanted them to be about 1.5 carats each. However, I asked myself WHY I wanted them and basically the answer was that it was because they were pretty, and shiny, and classic and went with every outfit (easy for travel). It was at that point that I realized they didn't have to be REAL diamonds, which would have cost between $5000 and $10000. Instead, I bought a good pair of fake ones (about $100.00) and they do the job just fine.

29. **Stop worrying about making other people uncomfortable**

I was invited to a party and everyone was selling something...wine, chocolates, clothes, etc...it was one of those online parties. And I'm making new friends and thought it might be nice to buy from them. But even a cheap item from both of them would have totaled almost 100 bucks! I had the money but I didn't need the stuff. I really hemmed and hawed over it and decided that I really didn't need them. My friends are still my friends, despite me not purchasing anything and I still have the money in the bank. And if you HAVE to purchase something, are they really friends? Or, are they just trying to make money off you?

30. Start with yourself and pull others along slowly with you.

My husband is a spender. When we first got married, I tried to make him a saver like me. It didn't work and a lot of disagreements ensued. Instead I just kept chunking along slowly, filling my clear Eiffel Tower jar with change and eventually he asked "what are you going to do with that money". I then explained and he said "that's cool." Now he makes it a game to save spare change in the Eiffel Tower with me and every time he gets a dollar bill, he stuffs it into his shoes to save up for vacation. It's not a lot but it is a start. That's all I can ask for. Also, he saves a portion of his paycheck to our savings acct each month. And I got him set up with a retirement account. Tiny actions.

31. Decide on Christmas presents early and purchase part of them each week.

I did this this year and it has been great! I decided to get my 3 nieces a "hot chocolate bar" for Christmas. So in November I started buying hot chocolate packets, marshmallows, toppings, mugs, etc... all told I probably spent 50-75 bucks on it but because I bought little things each week, it came out to 5-10 dollars in my normal grocery budget and so I didn't use my Christmas money on it and could instead use that on other things.

32. **Buy a gift card every time you go grocery shopping and use those for your Christmas/Holiday shopping.**

If you religiously spend money at a certain retailer, then every time you go grocery shopping, buy a gift card to that place. Then when holidays or birthdays come around, you can use those gift cards and you didn't deplete your current budget or your holiday budget.

33. **Think about maintenance, not just the initial purchase.**

My Grandpa Gray always used to say this. With a car-oil changes, tires, tune ups, car washes, new brakes, etc... These can be real budget busters if you have forgotten about them, so make sure to include them in. Same as when you are buying a house. Stick a maintenance category in your budget so that when you need a new washer and dryer, you aren't scrambling for money.

34. **Sell stuff online/consignment clothing store/Facebook marketplace/yard sale**

This is pretty self-explanatory. If you don't wear it or use it, get rid of it. Then use the money for something you really want!

35. Find a way to make more money at the job you currently have

As a teacher, I can make more money by adding duties to my day. I can cover other classes, supervise a lunch period, create lessons to sell on teachers-pay-teachers, coach, etc…Can you make more money at your job? Pick up extra shifts, work overtime, take on a new client during lunch, etc… It doesn't have to be forever, but it could help you boost your earnings for a short period of time.

36. Find a part time job that sells something you want

One of my friends took a job on weekends at World Market. She used the 50 percent off discount for employees to outfit her brand new home with brand new furniture. She worked there about 6 months, got the furniture and quit. Another friend, in Chicago, lost weight and wanted a whole new wardrobe. She worked at J Crew for about a year and a half. Again, used her employee discount to completely change her wardrobe and then she moved on. I have another friend that bartends on Saturday nights because she gets free alcohol while she works and half price food the rest of the time. Her husband joins her at the bar and so she makes money and enjoys herself.

37. Get out of debt and stay out of debt

Owing people money (bank, friends, family, etc…) means that you are paying today for yesterday's wants. The best way I know how to be present is to pay off your debt and they stay out of debt. Your money just seems to go farther when you don't have all these obligations to pay for.

38.   Invest early

If you have a job where the company enrolls you in a 401K or will match it. Spend a little time filling out the paperwork, put in $25.00 a paycheck and forget about it. I know that in your first job you want to keep as much money as you can. However, someday you will get older, and not want to work as much. If you have put away money, it will give you options for your future. Look at compounding interest, becoming a millionaire early, FIRE (Financial Independence, Retire Early). There are tons of books on money and investing.

39.   Use your raises and bonuses wisely.

Come up with a system that you put into practice every single time you receive a raise or bonus at work. I had a colleague that told me he would split the raise in half (let's say it was an extra 50 dollars a month.) He would save $25 and spend $25. He did this for 25 years and was able to retire very comfortably while also living comfortably during his working years. If you need the money badly, save 10 and keep 40 in your budget. Or save 5 and keep 45. 5 dollars a month doesn't seem like much but over a 25-year career, it can be a nice little chunk of change at the end.

40.   Do not spend money before you have it.

This seems like a no brainer but there are countless Hollywood movies that portray this exact tip. Usually the main character has spent the money they thought they were getting and when it doesn't happen, the rest of the movie entails them trying to get the money to pay for this expense. A lot of people do this with credit cards. I don't think credit cards are bad if you use them correctly. If you pay for an expense and then pay off the card, you are using it correctly. IF you pay for an expense and then HOPE the money that you are getting in a paycheck will cover it, you are setting yourself up for possible disaster.

41.   Simplify. Simplify. Simplify.

Read Walden by Henry David Thoreau. It shows how little we really have to have to exist. How many cups do you really need? How many shirts? How many plates? After reading this book, I look around and realized how much stuff I had that I didn't really use and didn't really need.

42.   Buy Quality

As a teacher I am on my feet all day and at the start of my career, I would wear these cute shoes that were probably from Payless or Walmart but they matched my outfit. You think you are saving money but in the long run, you aren't. I now own GOOD sandals, GOOD dressy boots and GOOD sneakers. My feet rarely hurt and I pay for that quality because it pays dividends later. I don't have any problems with my feet and a lot of teachers do.

43.   Learn what works for you.

It has taken me a long time to realize that you need to find what works for you and use it religiously. Don't let other people tell you that you are doing it wrong.

44.   Don't use the same system for every part of life.

I tried the moderation thing ($1.00 a day) for eating and I can't do it. So have to do the "no spend/no eat" instead. However, the moderation for my spending works quite well so I stick with that for money and stick with the other systems for food.

45.   Don't discount your own dreams to make someone elses come true

Selling parties have become a big thing lately. Buy this wine, this jewelry, this face cream, etc. They tell you to sell to your friends and for a while I would buy something from them. However, all those little purchases added up and I was sending them on cruises (top saleswoman) while not going on my own vacations. Once I realized that I was funding their dreams and not my own, I quickly stopped buying things I didn't need and started putting that money in a fund for myself.

46.   Can you combine two goals?

Can you combine a fitness goal and a money goal and make progress toward each of them at the same time? One of my friends really wanted to belong to a certain fitness studio but it was $100.00 a month and that was just not in her budget. So, she approached the manager and asked if there was any way around it. The manager said she could work the reception desk on Monday nights and then take classes for free on any other day. So she got paid AND she got to attend her fitness classes. Win-win! I worked at a summer camp that would essentially pay me to take kids on trips. I was able to white water raft, hike, go to Quebec, etc… for free because I was chaperoning my campers. I made money, got experience for teaching, AND was able to travel. It was awesome!

47.   It can't hurt to ask

I used to be embarrassed to ask for things. My parents had taught me that it was rude. However, as I get older I realize that people can't read your mind and the worst they can do is to say no so if you want something, ask for it. We were getting my husband a new cell phone. I was NOT planning on a new phone for myself. However, I had seen some promos for a new IPhone that were almost no cost to upgrade. During the sale of my husband's new phone, I simply asked the salesman about the promotion. He took my phone, looked it up, and told me that I could get a brand new one for only about $150.00 that day! Awesome! If I had never asked, I wouldn't have received the promotion and I would have gone back to the store 6 months later and had to buy the phone at full price. (about $1000.00) so one little question saved me $850.00!

48. Stock up on household supplies that can never expire

Toilet paper, paper towels, a particular body wash or deodorant, laundry detergent, kitty litter, salt for your water softener, etc…. When you have a little room in your budget, buy these things. Not food. And not something that you "might use." These are the tried and true, use them all the time, items. Then, the next week, if you need to buy meat or a bigger bill comes in, you don't also need toilet paper.

49. Have a signature wedding/graduation gift that you give to people.

My grandma used to do this. If you have a gift you ALWAYS give, then you can stock up for it all year round. She would "outfit your kitchen" with all the tools she thought were necessary to make meals. As soon as she received the news of the engagement, she would start her buying. Each week she would buy a different utensil (mixing spoon one week, measuring cups another week, parchment paper one week) Then at the wedding she had a giant basket of goodies and all her recipes. (Each week it only cost her a few extra dollars but at the wedding it looked like a very expensive and thoughtful gift)

Could you give them your grandma's amazing cookie recipe? Buy them all the ingredients for it and the pan they need to cook it? Or your mom's cheesy potato recipe and the crockpot for it? Something that in a pinch you could use? I like to give high school graduates a laundry basket, laundry soap, dryer sheets, Febreeze, etc…It is a practical gift and the items are something I can use if I don't get invited to any graduation parties. (That almost never happens)

50. Round up.

When I see that one of my savings accounts is $3.00 short of hitting $10.00 then I transfer $3.00. It's a fun little game to play and it makes me smile to have round numbers. I also pay bills that way. If the Mortgage is $1000.57. I add the other 43 cents to it and send it. Or I might add $9.43 to make it $1010.00 Every little bit counts.

51. Save up to pay large bills all at once and you can sometimes get a discount.

I just paid our car insurance for the next 6 months (instead of month to month) and it reduced my total bill by 140.00! Since it is an expense I have to pay anyway, I always pay it 6 months at a time to get this discount. Shop around and see if any other bills will give you a discount if you pay all at once.

52. $5.00/$1.00/quarter/dime game

There are multiple games on Pinterest that you can "challenge yourself to play." For example, the $5.00 bill game. When you pay in cash, every time you get a $5.00 bill, you put it aside and don't spend it. Then you save up all those $5.00 bills for another occasion. I saw online that a 2-liter bottle of pop holds $700.00 of dimes! My husband and I have been challenging ourselves to see if that is true and every dime we find; we add to the 2 liter. We aren't there yet, but I can't wait to see if it is true and that will be a nice chunk of change when we fill it!

53. Being organized saves money (razors/face cream/gift bags, food)

Last weekend I had to go to a party. Because I was organized, I found a blank card and envelope as well as a gift bag that I had left over from a tennis banquet. It saved me $5-7.00 and I didn't have to run to the store which was another bonus (saved gas!!). Another example of this is that all of my cheese is in one separate bin in the refrigerator. This way I know how much I have and it also never gets moldy because it doesn't get shoved into the back of the fridge and forgotten about.

54. Pay Bills/check accounts on a Friday (stops you from overindulging on weekend)

I learned this tip a few years ago. If I paid bills on a Monday, by Friday I would forget and indulge all weekend and then come Monday be sad. Instead, if I looked at things on Friday before the weekend, I knew how much I had or didn't have to spend.

55.   Use a 24 hour purchase pause. Or 36 hours or 48 hours

This goes along the same idea as a no spend but give yourself some time. If you are buying feverishly, you aren't thinking it through and should take some time to decide if those boots on sale are really necessary. After 24, 36, or 48 hours if you are still thinking about the boots, maybe you should go buy them. If you have forgotten about them, then leave them forgotten.

56.   Delay don't deny

Can you wait another 6 months? Can you wait until your bonus at work to buy something? Can you wait until Christmas or your birthday? If you can wait, you may find that you don't really need it or that your tastes have changed. Also, absence makes the heart grow fonder so you might really treasure the item if you wait a bit for it.

57.   Get rid of the "it has to be perfect" thoughts (candle vs diffuser)

I have a diffuser and essential oils that I really wanted once upon a time. I love burning candles. I'm almost out of the candle so I need to use the diffuser instead. It's not perfect but it will do. It will save me money and create less waste and still make my home smell great.

58.   Don't compete with friends or family members.

There is a reason that the phrase "Keeping up with the Joneses" exists and more recently it is "Keeping up with the Kardashians." You are NOT living their life; you are living yours. So, if your friend is buying fake lashes at $75.00 a pop and you can't because you are going on vacation, then call it what it is and grow up a little. Prioritize yourself and not others. I KNOW IT IS HARD, but if you want to succeed, you have to. Also, your friend might be massively in debt. Or maybe they have a trust fund. You cannot look at something that you think is similar to you and ask yourself, "Well I am just like them, I should be able to afford that too." No, you have to live your life. You have no idea what is going on behind the scenes in someone else's life. Here is an example from my own life. I had a friend who got a new car. I thought to myself, "I want a new car." However, this person NEVER goes on vacation. She pays $450.00 a month for this car. I LOVE traveling and $450.00 a month provides me the ability to take multiple nice vacations. All of a sudden, the new car didn't look so great and I went and washed my perfectly fine and paid for car. Two months later, I took a 5-day vacation to Las Vegas and she sat home with her car. Different priorities are FINE. However, you must realize this in order to succeed with money. I can't stress this enough.

Also, be careful of friends who are upgrading their homes/cars/etc…The little green monster of jealousy may creep up. It is ok. Realize it for what it is and then keep charging ahead to your own goals. I have a friend that just bought a really big house and for a small moment, I was jealous. Then after consideration I realized that she has not taken a vacation for over 5 years.

Chapter 4
Health

I am not a doctor. I am not a fitness trainer. I am just a working woman/wife who wants to keep her weight down, stay healthy and stay active. I have been able to reduce my A1c to the point of not being prediabetic. I am not on any medicines for cholesterol or triglycerides. I have been at a stable weight for the last few years. These tips have helped me achieve those health goals. Please consult your doctor before trying any of these tips.

1.   Wear pants with a button and zipper

2.   Sat- Wed or Mon-Fri

3.   One meal at a time (breakfast only healthy)

4.   Food journal

5.   Put groceries in trunk

6.   Consider a different exercise

7.   Use EVERYTHING YOU CAN! -death by 1000 cuts

8.   Drive by the gym

9.   Park far away

10.   Food out of sight

11.   Pack health snacks

12.   Sticker chart

13.   Step bet

14.   Too tight clothes

15.   Take pictures often

16.   Full length mirror

17.   Goal outfit

18.   No scale

19.   Store clothes that are too big/too small

20.   Find a good treat

21.   5-10 dinners to rotate

22.   Just one minute of exercise

23.   Leave 1-2 bites at every meal

24.   250 cals

25.   10 cals an hour

26.   Fitness tracker

27.   Drink water (one sip)

28.   Figure out your best time to exercise

29.   Take vitamins

30.   Keep adding a minute

31.   Become inefficient

32.   Eat the healthy foods you like

33. 1 piece of broccoli

34. Salad kit for lunch

35. Water not juice

36. Distract yourself (weights during cookie line)

37. No timeline for weight loss

38. Reduce coffee Creamer

39. No cheese/mustard not mayo

40. Add a banana

41. Don't always wear comfy clothes

42. Keep gym bag/sneakers in car

43. Ice in water

44. Wear workout clothes to bed

45. Avoid triggers (don't buy the cookies-buy 1 and eat it)

46. Assign a day to foods

47. Add in good before taking away bad

48. Save certain treats for certain times

49. Paint your nails

50. Use sheet therapy

1. Wear pants with a button and zipper

The first summer after freshman year of college, I worked at a summer camp in Maine and all I wore was stretchy shorts because they were our daily uniform. At the end of the 8 weeks, we had a special night in which I was supposed to wear the dress I bought. It didn't fit. I figured there must have been something wrong with the dress and didn't think too much about it until I arrived back in Michigan and none of my school clothes fit either. I had gained almost 15 pounds in 9 weeks. There were no scales and very few mirrors at this camp (it was an all-girls camp that wanted kids to focus on themselves and not their looks) so I had no idea that the dessert after every meal was packing the pounds on myself. The same thing happened to me during my first few years of teaching. I wore a lot of "stretchy waist" pants and started to gain weight.

I got tired of weighing myself daily. So this tip came in handy. Wear pants and skirts with buttons and zippers. You will know very quickly if you are gaining weight or not. I have a pair of gray pants that fit me or don't and if they don't, I know that it is time to eat healthier and move more.

2. Sat- Wed or Mon-Fri

A lot of health programs tell you to move 5-6 days a week and I always thought that meant Mon-Fri and rest on weekends. However, there are days of the week when I am teaching, that I am just purely exhausted. (Teach all day and parent/teacher conferences until 8 pm). So, I have learned to workout Saturday thru Wednesday. It works really well for me and it uses my energy on the weekends and Mon-Wed which is when I still have energy. It lets me rest on Thursday and Friday which is when I am most tired. Make working out work for you.

3.   One meal at a time (breakfast only healthy)

A lot of diets and healthy eating plans try to rehab your entire diet and exercise plan all at once. I take the approach of trying to eat one healthy meal a week, then one a day, then two a day and so on and so on. Go at your own pace and go slowly. Yes, you might not see the super-fast results of other diets but if the other diets worked, you wouldn't be reading this right now.

Research one healthy meal that you can make/cook/eat and then just eat that. Forget about diets and weight loss and the scale and all of that. Start with 1 meal. Then try 2. Then 3. You get the idea but if your diet is total crap food, just try eating one good meal. Let's say that you eat 21 meals a week and 7 snacks. So, 28 times a week that you make choices and put food into your mouth. Can you make one of them healthy?

4.   Food journal

You can't change what you don't know about. Write down what you eat so that you can tell areas where you might be able to make healthier choices. Today, I ate a graham cracker that was sitting on the counter as I cleaned up the dishes. By writing this down, next time I will make sure to get things out of sight.

5.   Put groceries in trunk

I have gone grocery shopping hungry which is a giant no no. I have also reached into the back seat or passenger seat and eaten a bunch of food before I have gotten home. Then I am not hungry for dinner. A small tip is to put your groceries out of reach as you drive. Then you can eat when you get home.

6.   Consider a different exercise

I love walking. It is my favorite form of exercise. However, when I golf, I consider that my exercise for the day. Or if I do a ton of yard work, I might consider that my exercise for the day. Be open to new types of exercise. You might be more active than you think you are!

7.   Use EVERYTHING YOU CAN! -death by 1000 cuts

I have learned to throw everything you can at a difficult goal. And I mean everything! The more tips and tricks I use, the healthier I seem to be. The idea behind this tip (and all of these tiny actions) is to keep making little bits of progress toward a goal so that you don't wake up one day with a house that is a mess, 20 pounds overweight, no money, etc…

8.   Drive by the gym

When I lived in Cincinnati, I joined a gym. There were two ways to get home from my school to my apartment. One way took me past the gym I joined. The other took me by a grocery store. Both were about the same amount of time. At first I would simply drive by the gym when I didn't feel like working out. Then I told myself I only had to go in and change my clothes. Then I told myself I only had to walk on the treadmill for 2 minutes, then 5 minutes. I built up my routine to 6 days a week, 20 min walk and 20 min treadmill. It was great. But that took weeks. Maybe even months. It all started with the small step of driving by the gym.

9.   Park far away

More steps make a difference. Park farther away from your destination. I am a teacher and I started parking in the farthest spot away from the door. It was about 100 extra steps one way. So 200 a day times 5 days a week. Every 2000 steps is a mile. So, I was walking an extra mile every two weeks. It seems silly right? But I was utilizing something I already had to do, which was go to work, and fitting in a few extra steps a day. One extra mile every two weeks? So, in a school year, that has me walking about 18 extra miles. Every little bit counts.

10.   Food out of sight

If you have to keep something in the house for some reason (like chocolate chips to make cookies), keep them out of sight as much as possible. I forgot we had half a bag of chocolate chips left over from Christmas because they were in the freezer behind vegetables. Therefore, they did not wind up in my stomach!

11.   Pack healthy snacks

I get super moody and unpleasant when I have not eaten. I now keep almonds and peanuts in every bag I carry. That way, I can eat something if we go to dinner and it is taking too long, or if I am stuck at school for a meeting, or whatever the reason may be that I can't get to an actual meal. It also helps me eat a proper meal when I finally get to sit down instead of eating way too much.

12.   Sticker chart

During the pandemic, I made a bullet journal of all the things that I wanted to work on and every time I did one of them, I would either color in a square or put a heart sticker in a box. It seems silly because I am 43 years old but it was super motivating and also very easy to tell what I had and had not accomplished that day. The pictures of this are on my website *tallgirltinysteps.com*

13.   Step bet

Join a competition. Some of my fittest days are when I am participating in a competition. I found stepbet online and it makes you pay an entry fee. If you keep up with your daily step goal, you get your money back plus you get to split whatever money that the people who dropped out put in. If you are a competitor, I highly recommend it. It hooks up to most fitness trackers and is super easy.

14.   14.Too tight clothes

Hear me out on this. I am not telling you to squeeze into really tight clothes every day and be miserable. But I have a pair of Cranberry colored Corduroy pants and they are a bit snug when I have been eating too much and working out too little. I wear them sometimes to remind myself that I don't need the extra calories in whatever it is I might choose to eat that day.

15.   Take pictures often

One of the best indicators of how you look is to take a picture. You can be sailing along thinking everything is going well and then you take a picture somewhere and wonder who the big girl is that is wearing your clothes. It can also be a great way to make you feel good if you have been working hard on your body and haven't seen much progress on the scale. You might take a picture and think, wow! I look pretty good!

16.   Full length mirror

You need to see what you look like. All of you. I know people that avoid mirrors because they don't like how they look. Buy a cheap mirror and give yourself a once over before you leave the house each day.

17.   Goal outfit

Keep an outfit around that you want to wear at your goal weight. This could be a swimsuit, wedding dress, or even a pair of pants that used to fit. Try this outfit on often. It will give you motivation when you feel like eating crappy food or just sitting around and not working out.

18.   No scale

I was my healthiest when I wasn't weighing myself. I hated that I might work out and eat healthy for weeks only to see the scale not move or even go up. If you gauge your weight with your pants that button, you don't need a scale that says you went up 5 pounds or down 5 pounds. A lot of times the scale would just discourage me and I would give up my healthy habits or working out because I didn't see "progress." Now, I measure progress in other ways and don't bother with the scale.

19. Store clothes that are too big/too small

You are where you are right now. Accept it. Do NOT have clothes in your closet that don't fit you. It used to upset me in the morning when I looked longingly at those clothes and wished for a different body. I have some really cool clothes that I am not ready to part with. Therefore, I bought some storage containers and I folded them up and kept them in there. Maybe someday I will get rid of them but I want to keep them for the time being. However, they don't need to be in my current closet. (One example is a wool suit I bought when I lived in Paris)

20. Find a good treat

Some days you just need a treat. I have found two things that are a small treat and they help me stay on track toward a healthy lifestyle. In the summer, it's vanilla pudding. In the winter, it's hot chocolate. Both treats are under 100 calories but they satisfy my cravings and keep me going on the right path.

21. 5-10 dinners to rotate

I hate thinking about dinner. It used to stress me out in a major way. Now I have 5-10 dinners that are easy to cook, easy to shop for and healthy and I rotate them each week. It has made a world of difference!

22.   Just one minute of exercise

This one is huge if you want to get back into exercising (or start for the first time) and you don't know how or you don't think you can. Do 1 minute. I did this in the winter time when exercise seemed almost impossible. I told myself that I only had to complete 1 minute on the elliptical and as soon as I did it, I congratulated myself and hopped off and went about my night. I did this for a few weeks and then moved up to 2 minutes, 3 minutes and so on and so forth. Now I take daily walks but I had to build up to that. So many programs tell you to exercise for 30-45 minutes, 5 days a week. If you aren't there, you aren't there! MIND THE GAP! This is a huge one for knowing your starting place and then acting accordingly. It is so much better to go slowly at first and stick with something than to go full blast and quit after a month.

23.   Leave 1-2 bites at every meal

If you are not ready for a full on diet change, continue to eat what you always have but do not clean your plate. Leave a few bites on your plate at every meal. This could easily cut 100-200 calories a day without much work! One way to do this is to scoop a small part of your meal to the side and dump a bunch of salt on it or put it on the bread plate. Get it away from you! Then when you finish your meal, you are done.

24.   250 cals

At the beginning of my sophomore year of college, I was heavy. I had gained 15 pounds during the school year and put on another 10-15 over the summer. The idea of dieting has always rubbed me the wrong way. However, I read somewhere that losing a pound a week is just cutting out 250 calories a day and exercising 250 calories more a day. This seemed doable. I could ride my bike to class instead of taking the bus and I could cut out cheese and mayonnaise on my sandwich every day. Boom! It started to work in the first week and I was able to lose 25 pounds that year. I never felt deprived and I still enjoyed pizza and beer like a college kid, but I was able to shed the weight and feel so much better.

25.   10 cals an hour

This goes with the above tip. Could you burn an extra 10 calories an hour? If you can, you will burn 250 more a day. I am still working on this tip but one idea was leg raises or walking to a bathroom that is farther away at work.

26.   Fitness tracker

This one is huge for me. Sometimes I think I am working really hard and spending a lot of energy and then I look at my Fitbit and I realize that I don't have as many steps as I thought I did. It is very eye opening and helps me to "add a few steps" when I see that I have not moved much throughout the day. I have also been increasing my step count slowly each week to try to get in better shape. Actual numbers help me to do that.

27.   Drink water (one sip)

About 2 years ago, I didn't really like to drink water. I know how good it is for you and I just didn't really want to drink water. I can't explain why. However, I would be proud of myself if I could just drink one sip. That's it. One sip. I have slowly been able to increase that to a few glasses of water per day.

28.   Figure out your best time to exercise

I hate changing my clothes and showering. Once I have done it for the day, I don't want to change them again or take a second shower. So my best time to exercise is in the morning, right as I roll out of bed. Then I shower and get ready for the day. I used to try to make myself exercise at night and I always came up with excuses as to why I couldn't or I was too tired or I didn't want to get sweaty or whatever it was. So now, my perfect day is to have a cup of coffee, walk and then shower and get ready. Do what works for you!

29.   Take vitamins

A lot of people swear by vitamins. A lot of people think they are worthless. I figure they can't hurt. I take a multi-vitamin, vitamin C and just started Biotin because I'm growing out my hair. My husband swears that Biotin is making his hair grow so we will see.

30.   Keep adding a minute

Anything you don't like doing, see if you can just add one minute. I do this with exercise. If I walk for 30 minutes on Tuesday, I try to walk for 31 minutes on Wednesday. Then 32 minutes on Thursday.

31.   Become inefficient

So, to get more steps in, become INEFFICIENT. Here is an example. Let's say I have 4 loads of laundry to do and my washing machine is in the basement. EFFICIENCY would say to carry everything down there, do it all, then when it's all done, carry it back up. INEFFICIENCY means that I walk one load down, put it in the washer, walk back up. Then when it needs the dryer, I walk the second load down, switch them out and walk the first load back up. Guess what this gives me? 8 trips up and down stairs (then I don't have to go to the gym).

32.　Eat the healthy foods you **DO** like

I know you are supposed to eat a well-rounded diet with lots of fruits and vegetables. I don't like vegetables. Or at least I never liked the vegetables my mom wanted to feed me (carrots, cauliflower, lima beans-YUCK!) However, I love mushrooms, tomatoes, and cucumbers. So instead of feeling badly about the stuff that I don't like to eat, I simply eat the vegetables and fruits that I DO like. I figure that it's better than nothing. And better than potato chips.

33.　1 piece of broccoli

I HATE broccoli. However, I had hyperthyroidism (that is now in remission) and eating broccoli was very important in that healing process. I would have to choke it down on a daily basis. So I told myself that I only had to eat one piece. Not a whole cup of it, not a whole stalk of it. One piece. And I did that. For 2 years straight. Is there some food that you know you should eat but you just don't want to? Can you eat one little piece of it? Kind of like when we were kids and your parents would say, "ok, you can leave the table if you just eat two more bites."

34.　Salad kit for lunch

I pack my lunches for school (teacher) and I have discovered something called a salad kit. It comes with the lettuce, dressing, cheese, black pepper and croutons. I LOVE IT. So, first of all, it is two servings but only 400 calories so I eat both servings. The second part that I love is that I only have about 25 minutes to eat and it takes me about that long to eat the whole thing (soup is the same way) so it keeps me busy all of lunch and I am not as tempted to grab a cookie or other snack that someone has brought into the teacher's lounge.

35.   Water not juice

A lot of diet plans tell you to not drink your calories. One of the easiest switches for me was to drink water instead of juice. Juice is very caloric and a nice treat sometimes but it can really pack on the pounds and sugar if you drink it every day.

36.   Distract yourself (weights during cookie line)

Sometimes you just need good ole fashion distraction to avoid eating something that is not great for you. When I worked at the summer camp, they had something called cookie line every day. A fresh warm cookie and carton of milk. It was glorious! However, it was also packing the pounds on me the first summer I was there. So the next summer, I devised a plan. I would eat a cookie on Sundays only. Then every other day during cookie line (20 min) I would walk to the gym, do 1 set of hand weights, and walk back. No one really missed me (350 campers and 150 staff) and my close friends understood that I needed to fill my time so that I could button my pants at the end of the summer! It worked! I LOVED Sundays when I enjoyed a cookie with everyone and I liked the days that I distracted myself. Sometimes I didn't even lift weights. I would just walk to the gym. Sit in the quiet for a few minutes, and walk back. It was enough time to "miss the cookies" and keep myself on the right track.

37. No timeline for weight loss

If you know that you have to "Lose 10 pounds by Friday" you resort to some pretty drastic measures. The best thing I have done is to not give myself a timeline for weight loss. That helps me in 2 ways. One, then I am never really "finished" and I don't go "off my diet" and two, it helps keep me sane when I do slip up or I'm not progressing as quickly as I think I should.

38. Reduce Coffee Creamer

I used to go through a coffee mate flavored creamer container about once a week. I loved it. For the longest time, I thought I couldn't live without it. So instead of giving it up cold turkey, which is what diet books tell you to do, I reduced it down very very very slowly. So instead of just pouring it in, I measured it. Then instead of 3 tablespoons I did 2 and ¾. Then 2 and ½. Then 2 and ¼. Then when I got all the way down to 1 Tablespoon, I switched to almond milk creamer but that made me want more so I went away from that. Then I would put in 1 tablespoon of sugary flavored creamer and 1 tablespoon of half and half. I reduced that down to my current 1 tablespoon per cup of plain powder creamer. THIS PROCESS TOOK YEARS!!!!!!!!! And I am so glad I stuck with it but just know that it is OK for something that you love to take a long time to work on. (I can't have artificial sweeteners so that was never an option)

39.   No cheese/mustard not mayo

Can you make small substitutions that you barely recognize? And maybe not even every day? Like leaving cheese off your sandwich or burger? Maybe only on Tuesday and Thursday if you eat a sandwich every day? Or maybe just on Fridays? Choosing mustard over mayonnaise? Adding Avocado and tomato and lettuce instead of mayo? Switching from 2 percent milk to 1 percent? Drink half diet coke and half regular coke (my husband does this with fountain pop) Water down your hot chocolate? Put ice in your sweet tea so that you don't ingest as many calories but you got to "have your drink." Try to make it a game to see where you can cut a few calories each day.

40.   Add a banana

Carry a banana or apple with you everywhere. Eat it. Remember, these are just little tiny actions to improve your health. A banana or apple is ALWAYS better than a bag of chips or a candy bar.

41.   Don't always wear comfy clothes/leggings

Athleisure has done us a disservice. We THINK that we are looking tight and right and working out. Until we get into a pair of jeans or pants with a button and wonder what happened. You HAVE to get dressed sometimes. Even if you don't work outside the home. The small step of making an effort with your outfit, leads to other small steps. Trust me. I have a friend who works from home and doesn't even wear real pants anymore (its only leggings). Aside from the aesthetics of getting bigger, I can't believe that she is that healthy either.

42.   42.Keep gym bag/sneakers in car

When I was a tennis coach, I always had a gym bag and sneakers in my car in case a kid needed something. However, it also came in handy when I was early for a meeting and could get some steps in. One time I was about 30 minutes early to a state seeding meeting and so I walked on the track until the meeting started. I had worn flip flops but luckily I had my shoes and socks in the car and got about 2 miles in. If I hadn't had the proper shoes, I would have just sat in my car on my phone. This was a much better use of my time.

43.   Ice in water

I found that drinking water with ice in it, gets me to drink more water. As a teacher I would take a water bottle to school and it would get warm and I wouldn't drink it. Now, I fill my tumbler with ice only and fill up water at school. I also really like a metal straw and a tumbler like a YETI that keeps it cold all day long.

44. Wear workout clothes to bed

I hate changing my clothes. I don't know why but I just do. So I will wear my workout clothes to bed (t-shirt and shorts) and put my sneakers and socks right by the door to my basement. Then I simply get up, put my shoes on and start walking on the treadmill. I won't lie, some mornings I do the first 3-5 minutes without even opening my eyes.

45. Avoid triggers (don't buy the entire package of cookies-buy 1 and eat it)

I LOVE girl scout cookies. But I have learned that I cannot eat "just a few" and save the rest. I eat an entire sleeve of thin mints in one sitting. So this year, I didn't buy any. None. Not one box. I did go to a restaurant where they were selling them outside. I bought one box and split it with a friend so I only brought home one sleeve. So much better than what I used to do (5-6 boxes)

If you have something that you can't hold back on, buy one, enjoy it and move on. I cannot buy a box of cookies or a bag of Hershey Kisses. I will eat them all. Therefore, I buy a single chocolate bar, eat the whole thing and then am done for a while.

46. Assign a day to foods

If cooking and meals stress you out, assign a certain type of dish to a certain day of the week. Think Taco Tuesday! My friend does

Chicken Mondays, Taco Tuesdays, Whitefish Wednesdays, Takeout Thursdays, French Fridays. It makes it fun and keeps her organized.

47. Add in good before taking away bad

A lot of diets are very restrictive. I like to add in healthy items before I take away unhealthy items. It helps me to not feel deprived and then I am too full to eat the bad items. One example is fruit. I add in fruit as a snack before I forbid myself to eat potato chips or junk food.

48. Save certain treats for certain times (like ALWAYS eat pie on Thanksgiving but not at other times. Only have ice cream in summer.

I live in Michigan. I only eat ice cream in June, July and August. I only eat apple cobbler in October when the apples are fresh. I only eat Christmas cookies in December. Chocolate candies in February. By having little rules like this, it lets me indulge in the fun of the season/holiday but also sets up some restrictions that naturally help keep my weight down. Yes, I have been offered ice cream in December and I politely decline. Chocolate candy is messy and melty in the summer so I don't eat it then.

49. Repaint your nails (or some other task that keeps your hands occupied)

I repaint my nails on Sunday nights. However, if I feel like I really want to snack one night, I might repaint them earlier so that it keeps my hands busy and occupied. I usually forget about the snack after waiting an hour or so for my nails to dry.

50. Use sheet therapy (go to bed)

When all else fails, go to bed. You probably need sleep and if all you can think about is food at 8 pm…just go to bed. They call this sheet therapy in AA.

Chapter 5
Work and School

I am a high school teacher. I have worked in jobs without kids, (curtain rod factory/ Jimmy John's sandwiches) but for the majority of my life, my jobs have been with kids so a lot of these tips are centered around teaching or school. However, some of them are generic enough that you could use them for any occupation (like putting out your outfit the night before or clearing your desk before you arrive each day.)

1.   Clear desk before leaving each day
2.   Arrive early
3.   Set purse/backpack by the door each night (fully packed)
4.   Pack lunch ahead of time
5.   Top off gas tank whenever weather is good
6.   Use spare moments (grade papers in hallway)
7.   Outfit the night before
8.   Know your productive times
9.   BE specific when asking for things from others (email/in person)
10.   Get experience before your job
11.   Be honest about your effort level
12.   PUT AWAY YOUR PHONE
13.   Something is always better than nothing
14.   Go smaller

15. Organization and simplicity

16. Increase by 1 minute (concentration/studying, etc.)

17. Wear comfortable shoes

18. Always have snack with you

19. Find an app or game that can help you (calendar/duolingo, podcast)

20. At work, work. At home, rest.

21. BE prepared (laptop/notebook/pen, etc…)

51. 22 Have a uniform that looks good and professional

52. 23 Have an interview outfit always

53. 24. Check the weather (help kids learn to check the weather)

54. 25. Read

55. 26. Always keep learning (even if it isn't directly related to your "day job")

56. 27. Take advantage of ANY training that work provides you

Then, a parent section (a few tips for parents to help their kids)

1. Clear desk before leaving each day

During the day, your work desk can get messy and sometimes you just want to get out of your job and go home. Take the few minutes to tidy up before you leave. It makes a world of difference when you arrive in the morning and if you want to be super productive, make a list of the first 3 things you should do when you get to work the next day.

2.   Arrive early

There is no excuse to be late. I'm sorry, that may sound harsh but if you can be on time at the airport for a vacation, you can be on time to work. Any time you arrive somewhere early, it gives you a chance to use the restroom, get yourself together, fix any problems that may pop up, etc… I have had colleagues that would show up to school about 10 minutes before the kids and then they wondered why they had to "take work home with them" and they felt like they could never get everything done. Well, you started your day in a rush and it didn't slow down from there. In my experience, the day always speeds up until you get home, eat dinner and relax.

3.   Set purse/backpack by the door each night (fully packed)

I cannot believe how many students (and adults) don't do this. I am a decent morning person. However, even I forget things in the morning and then get to school only to realize I don't have something. And if you oversleep? Forget about it! So pack everything the night before-laptop, snack, keys, wallet, glasses, extra sweater, workout clothes, etc…IF you have to charge your laptop, plug it in RIGHT NEXT TO YOUR BAG! I can't tell you how many students forget their computers because "they are charging in my bedroom". Oh really? Your bedroom that is dark and messy and you could barely find your way out of this morning? Of COURSE, you forgot it! Adults, do better. You know what you need on a daily basis. And help your kids/spouse! You probably know what they need also.

4.   Pack lunch ahead of time

Here is another one just like the bag. Put as much stuff as you can in your lunch bag the night before. OR, take something like soup that doesn't need to be refrigerated. Make your sandwich the night before. Throw in your protein bar. Whatever it is, do as much as possible the night before so you aren't stumbling in the morning.

5.   Top off gas tank whenever weather is good

I live in Michigan and the weather is very temperamental. We have a saying "if you don't like the weather, just wait 5 minutes" So whenever the weather is good, I try to top off my gas tank. Because there will be days that are snowing, raining, sleeting, 95 degrees and you just don't want to get out of your nice car once you get into it. ALWAYS have gasoline, DO not be that person that runs close to empty, that is just setting up your day for disaster.

6.   Use spare moments (grade papers in hallway)

One lovely part of teaching is that you are expected to be in the hallway (monitoring students) while classes change. It is about a 4-6-minute period where kids switch classes. Some people stand in the hallway and chit chat with kids or other teachers. I use this time to grade (if I am behind on grading). You may say "well you can't get much done in that time". That is true. Depending upon the assignment (usually a 5-

10 question one) I can only complete 5 or so. However, in a high school you change classes 5-6 times a day and if you get 5 done each hour, that is one class that is finished by the end of the day! Remember, these are little ways to make your life easier. (And yes I still sit down in silence to grade essays)

7. Outfit the night before

I really thought everyone already did this. You need to pick out your outfit the night before. Make sure you have everything for it…the right bra, underwear, shoes, shirt, belt, pants, etc… Yes I know that you could just pick it out in the morning but my husband is a hot mess when he tries to do this in the morning. He is way calmer when he picks it out the night before. (there is nothing worse than running around the house searching for your brown belt when you were supposed to be out the door 5 minutes ago). It also gives you a chance to inspect for stains/rips/wrinkles/etc… And if you have kids, PLEASE do this with them also. Get them in the habit-it makes the mornings go so much smoother.

8. Know your productive times

I am kind of worthless after 3pm. My best work times are between 6am and noon. My husband is the opposite. He struggles in the morning and is much better at night. Learn this about yourself and then try to do as much as possible during your productive time. This is another reason I get to school early. I am awake and focused. By 3pm I have used up all my patience and concentration for the day.

9. Be specific when asking for things from others (email/in person)

My husband taught me this. Don't hem and haw around things. Ask for what you want/need and move on. Everyone is busy. Get to the point.

10. Get experience before your job

Before I became a teacher, I was in Big Brothers/Big Sisters, a babysitter, a camp counselor, a substitute teacher, a classroom volunteer, a tennis instructor. By the time I got to my actual classroom, I had worked with kids so long that it felt normal. I was also offered two teaching jobs the minute I left college. ALSO, I use some of my camp counselor tips to quiet down a room (even 20 years later). Get as much experience as you can for the job you think you want. I know people that get to their first year of teaching, realize they hate kids, and then have to find a different career. Not the greatest idea.

If you want to go into banking, see if you can do an internship or job shadow. Interview bankers. Talk to people about finance. If you want to go into law, same thing. Any career has multiple opportunities that you can try out and see if you like that lifestyle/career. I know a girl that started working at a coffee shop in high school. She fell in love with it. She is taking business classes and also managing the shop and one day wants to own a franchise. You never know where a part time job will take you. I know another person that volunteered in a flower shop because she thought it would be cool. Yes, there were cool parts of it but ultimately she learned she didn't like "running a business" and so she has taken a different path.

11.   Be honest about your effort level

Are you really trying as hard as you say you are? Or do you get to work and then check Facebook/Instagram/talk to coworkers/walk the halls/etc.? I had a colleague that would get to work TWO HOURS ahead of everyone else. One day my power was out at home so I went to school to get ready. I saw him there and I observed him. He did EVERYTHING BUT WORK! And he always complained about being behind. If you can learn to use your time wisely, it will really pay off in the amount of work you get done and how much free time you have.

12.   PUT AWAY YOUR PHONE

It is distracting. In any job and in any situation. If at all possible, put your phone away and check it on breaks or at lunch.

13.   Something is always better than nothing

This one is hard for people. A lot of times it is better to do something than nothing at all. For example, in teaching, I may want to accomplish 15 things during a lesson but the students only grab on to one. It seems disappointing but they learned SOMETHING and that is better than nothing! Also, if you get to work and can only finish one project, it is better to finish that one project than to have 3 unfinished ones. I tell my students all the time that one paragraph is better than a blank piece of paper. And two paragraphs are better than one and so on and so forth.

14.   Go smaller

If something seems overwhelming or impossible, then you have to go smaller. At work and school, if you can't get your whole assignment completed, can you get one section of it completed? Yes, I know this isn't ideal but I can't tell you how many kids will not even start their work because they don't think they can get it all done. They would be much better served in the long run if they could just do a little bit of it and eventually work up to the entire assignment.

15.   Organization and simplicity

If your desk is usually a mess. Can you focus one minute a day on filing papers, throwing away trash, stacking important papers, etc…? I am a better teacher when everything is organized. Students do better when their notebooks and folders are organized. That doesn't stop just because you became an adult and "got a real job."

16.   Increase by 1 minute (concentration/studying, etc.)

A LOT of students want to be good at school and they are told that if they just study more or have better goals, they can achieve it. I am here to call you out a little bit on that. If you can't sit still for one minute, you can't study for 30. So start with one minute. The next night 2 minutes and so on and so forth. If you are a parent of a child in school, help them with this. Time them. Make it a game. You have to do some teaching at home. Study techniques are a lost art and schools just don't always have time to teach them. Help your child figure out what they need to be successful (headphones, breaks, silence, a desk, etc...) and then get them those things! I didn't learn (until college) that I could NOT study at my dorm room or house. I needed the library or a coffee shop. I would even study in the dining hall. I just couldn't be near all the distractions of laundry, TV, friends, etc...

17.   Wear comfortable shoes

People are pretty worthless when their feet hurt. Wear appropriate, yet comfortable shoes.

18.   Always have snack with you

People are also worthless when they are hungry. Keep a healthy snack with you at all times. A little package of nuts can save you from a meltdown if a meeting runs long, the cafeteria runs out of food, etc...

19. Find an app or game that can help you (calendar/duolingo, podcast)

My husband and I have a shared digital calendar. I study French on the Duolingo app. I wrote this book on Google Docs so that I can access it anywhere. Find tools/apps/games that make it fun, interesting and easy.

20. At work, work. At home, rest.

Enough said. And checking your work email is not rest.

21. Be prepared (laptop/notebook/pen, etc…)

For the love of all things, if you don't show up prepared, you are already starting off on the wrong foot. AT LEAST have a notebook and a pen. I see so many students that stroll into class with no supplies, sit there and then can't get to work because they didn't bring a writing utensil. COME ON! You have to try a little bit!

22. Have a uniform that looks good and professional

Whatever industry you work in, you know what is appropriate for your daily attire. Make sure you have that and wear it often. I am not saying to spend a bunch of money, especially if this is your first job, but look up a capsule wardrobe and buy a few pairs of pants and shirts that are interchangeable. DO NOT wear your college clothes to your first job. In the appendix of this book is an example of my "outfit list" that is slightly capsule wardrobe and slightly some other clothes. I put the date next to the outfit when I wear it so that I know what I have worn before and also if I need to discard clothes (never choose them) or purchase different clothes (black skirt) to add to the outfit combination.

23.   Have an interview outfit always

Even if you love your job, you should have an interview outfit that fits and is ready at a moment's notice. You never know when you might be called by a headhunter or for a promotion and you can't walk in there looking like a slob. Also, my interview outfit is a shirt and skirt that I wear to school and then a blazer I keep looking nice just in case. Also, regularly, make sure it fits, is clean, and unwrinkled. There is nothing worse than trying to find shoes for an outfit the night before an interview. Use that time for sample questions, a healthy dinner and relaxation so that you are at your best.

If you are just coming out of college and can't afford an interview outfit, borrow something from a friend/parent, go to Goodwill or charge it on your credit card. Men, you need a suit. Women, skirt and jacket or pants and jacket with an acceptable, non-revealing shirt underneath. You are better to be overdressed for an interview than underdressed. Also, dress "one notch above" what you would typically wear in the job. So, if it is a factory position where you would wear jeans and a t-shirt every day, you should interview in dress pants and a dress shirt. If it is a banking position where you would wear dress pants and a dress shirt/polo shirt each day, then you need to wear a suit. My father had a kid come in to his office in flip flops to apply for a heavy machinery factory job. He didn't even interview the kid. The next kid came in to his office in khaki pants, steel toed work boots and a polo shirt tucked in. My dad said he knew he was going to hire him immediately because the kid showed that he understood the job.

Also, be aware of the community in which you are interviewing. If everyone went to Harvard Law School, then you better look and dress like Harvard Law School. Even teaching jobs can vary by community. I am not saying to wear farm clothes to a school in a farming community. Instead, I am merely telling you to be aware of your surroundings so that you can dress appropriately.

24. Check the weather (help kids learn to check the weather)

Being too hot or too cold is uncomfortable. Learn to check the weather and dress accordingly. Bring an umbrella. Wear sunscreen.

25. Read

Learn from others. Be educated. And no, quotes on Instagram doesn't count. Have something to talk about with your colleagues other than what happened on "The Bachelor" last night. Many interviews will ask what book you are currently reading. Have something to tell them.

26. Always keep learning (even if it doesn't seem related to your "day job")

This year I have studied French and personal finance. I don't know if I will ever use these things in my actual career but they help me to know more about the world and knowing more is always a good thing.

27. Take advantage of ANY training that work provides you

Last year my school offered free CPR training. I took the class and am now CPR certified. I don't know if I will never use it/need it but it is a good skill to have. Take advantage of any additional training that your job wants to send you to or pay for. You never know when you might need it for a different job or a promotion within your own company.

Parent Section

Parents-Please keep helping your teenagers. Teach your kids how to clean out their school bags. Help them get organized each day and week. Get the bag ready for school on Monday. I know this isn't fun and you would rather have family time doing something else, but these small actions can make a big difference in the success of your child.

1.   Make sure homework is done for the night/week.

2.   Assess your kid's organization and see if they need help

3.   Clean out any food/utensils/etc…

4.   Get ready for the week…this is a great time to discuss the week coming up. Kids DON'T just automatically do this. They just don't. YOU HAVE TO TEACH THEM. AND ESPECIALLY TEENS. THEY NEED TO BE TAUGHT! My freshman in high school are TERRIBLE at having their stuff, checking due dates, etc…

5.   Get their outfit and bag ready for Monday-a lot of my students are like "I forgot my Chromebook". When you go to bed you should have everything by the door ready to leave. If things need to be charged then plug them in by their school bags. Keys/lunch/coffee/purse/   uniform/sports   stuff/etc…It REALLY makes a difference with your kids at school.

6.   Look at the weather-no kid likes to be cold, wet, or too hot.

7.   Make sure they have lunch money/lunch

8.   CONTROL THE CELL PHONE. So many issues arise from social media, cell phone usage, etc. PLEASE be the "meanie" and limit your child's cell phone usage. It will help everything.

9.   Get your child involved in something at the school. (sports, clubs, music, plays) It makes it more fun for them and they tend to do better in their studies when they like coming to school each day.

10. Check grades and email teachers. Even for your senior in high school. So many parents say "well they are an adult now so it is on them." No they aren't. They are still babies. They are even

babies at 18. Help them. Parent them. Check on them. They want you to. Believe me. Even if they fight you on it, they want to know that you care and are paying attention. I have taught teens (in one way or another) for over 25 years and they still need our help, no matter how mature they seem.

Chapter 6
Home

This one for me is the creme de la creme. I feel as though I have done the most work on this section of the book. I have researched, studied, read, experimented and have given you all the tips that help keep my household together so that I do NOT have to spend my nights and weekends keeping things picked up or clean. It is also the section that goes bad very quickly if I don't do these little actions regularly.

1. Pull comforter up/put in front of closet

2. Wash lunch dishes at school/work

3. Wash dishes/put away dishes while coffee brews (use little moments)

4. Organize pantry one shelf at a time

5. Use cardboard boxes and label things in your pantry

6. Clean out car when get gas or go through car wash (always keep small trash bag inside car)

7. Slide clothes to other end of closet after you wear them

8. Use your stuff up

9. Have people over

11.   Always carry something with you to another room

12.   Declutter one/5/10 things a day

13.   Count number of seconds it takes and make it a game

14.   Clear one surface

15.   One is enough

16.   Don't waste valuable real estate for storage

17.   Keep cleaning supplies in the room they are used (and keep them out)

18.   Always have a Dopp kit packed

19.   Make piles

20.   Have a dump room

21.   Buy sterilite drawers and have kids set out a Monday-Friday in each drawer

22.   Reconsider where you store things

23.   Dump clean laundry on bed

24.   Bra, underwear, sock drawer-deodorant on top of that dresser

25.   Switch out seasons

26.   Cleaning lady

27.   Move to right location (deodorant in bedroom)

28.   Put at top or bottom of stairs

29.   Make a place for blankets/remotes

30.   Hook instead of chair

31.   Day bin and night bin in bathroom

32. Washcloth to clean out sink at night

33. Towel not a bathmat

34. Christmas mugs and clothes with Christmas decor

35. Pattern socks

36. Separate laundry baskets for diff family members or colors

37. Don't fold socks

38. 1 load a day

39. Dishwasher every night before bed

40. Little kids wash and dry and KEEP IN BASKETS

41. Lingerie bag for socks and undies

42. Sheet set-1 to wear and 1 while cleaning. Same with towel (Can always buy more) (unless special needs or baby)

43. Unpack 1-2 things a day from car/bag/backpack/moving box/etc…

44. Lazy Susan in cupboards and fridge.

45. Keep backstock somewhere else

46. Trash can every room

47. Upstairs/downstairs vacuum

48. Use dead time (Tv time at night to fold laundry/clean out purse/etc…)

49. Make a chart of all possible outfits

50. Fold laundry while on the phone

51. Have zones for the things you don't like to do (socks)

52. Have a funeral outfit

53. Separate clothes into zones for their function (golf, work, workout, etc.)

54. One towel color for each family member that matches their sheets

55. One sock brand for each kid (under armour/Nike) or draw initial on toes

56. Command center near door (pens/scissors/tape/)

57. Color Code your closet

58. Toothpaste in sink

59. Clean before vacay

60. Keep "sometimes things" all in one spot-swimsuit bag

61. Buy a baby crockpot

62. Fold laundry while on phone

1. Pull comforter up.

I see and read all the books about making your bed in the morning and I love them. I have tried it. However, it doesn't work for me. I get out of bed first before my husband. By the time I get back into the bedroom after my shower, I am already in "get dressed mode" so I pull up the comforter. I don't arrange the pillows. I don't fold any extra blankets (we live in Michigan and keep the house cool at night in the winter). If we are having company, I will strip the bed, fold everything nicely, put the pillows in a Pinterest worthy arrangement, etc…But my tiny tip is to just pull the comforter up. It keeps it off the floor which immediately makes the bedroom look cleaner.

2.   Wash lunch dishes at school/work.

I am a high school teacher who sometimes only gets 25 minutes to scarf down lunch. It is barely enough time to walk to the lunch room, wait for the microwave (see tip 60 for buying a baby crockpot) scarf down the food in about 15 minutes so that I can use the restroom (because I can't leave a class of kids unattended during a class) and hustle back to my classroom and prepare to teach a group of rowdy kids (they are always rowdy after lunch). BUT, I have found that if I wash out my lunch dishes in the staff lounge when I am done (usually takes about 2 minutes) then when I get home I am in a MUCH better mood.

I take out my ice pack and throw it back in the freezer, set the dishes beside the sink to use the next morning and stick my lunch cooler up above my coffee cabinet. Easy peasy.

In contrast, let me show you how it goes if I DON'T wash out my dishes. 1. I get home and take the dishes out of my lunch bag. They sat all day so they are crusty. I fill them with soap and water to soak. I forget about them or am too tired to worry about them. Then the next morning I grab more Tupperware all the while being mad that there are still dishes in the sink. Repeat for 5 days and you have a mountain of coffee cups and dishes in the sink that are now slightly gross and need quite a bit of attention. (And that scenario assumes that you live alone and it is only your dishes in the sink)

3.   Wash dishes/put away dishes while coffee brews (use little moments)

One morning, I was standing half asleep in front of my coffee maker as it brewed and I looked over at the sink. I had yesterday's coffee mug and spoon still sitting there. Why you might ask? I don't know. I was probably too tired to deal with it the day before. So I grabbed the soap scrub brush, washed and rinsed them and set them on the counter before my coffee had brewed. As I rejoined the living that morning, I challenged myself to always USE the coffee brewing time to clean something in the kitchen. One morning I wiped down the counters. Another morning I unloaded half the dishwasher. One morning I folded kitchen towels I had just washed. Another morning I wiped out the sink with a cleanser. Another morning I threw away some expired food in the refrigerator. Nothing earth shattering but it helps keep the kitchen clean.

My mother, God love her, waits until she has an entire sink of dishes before she does any of them. If that method works for you, keep at it. However, a lot of times she has dishes drying all over the kitchen (hand wash items) and the dishwasher going AND there are dishes she didn't get to. She was a stay at home mom and this system worked for her. I don't have that time or the patience so I use the tiny coffee brewing moments.

4.   Organize pantry one shelf at a time

I LOVE Pinterest. I LOVE watching the Home Edit on Netflix. But too often I would watch these things, get super inspired, rip everything out of my cupboard, tell myself I needed matching bins, go to the store, come home, lose my motivation, do a couple of bins and then just shove everything right back in because dinner was starting soon and I didn't have time to deal with stacking the taco seasoning in rainbow order. So it started with an Amazon box. It was the perfect size for my pantry. I took EVERY granola bar/breakfast bar that I could find and threw them into this box. I then wrote "breakfast bars" in black Sharpie and put it back into the cupboard. Before that we had about 6 different boxes that contained 1 or 2 bars each in them and it was taking up a ton of space. Plus, when I would go to the store, I didn't know what we needed.

After that part looked so good, I found another small box I had and put every seasoning pocket we had in it. It wasn't quite as magical as the breakfast bars but it worked. Then I quit. Those two things took about 2 minutes and I didn't make a mess of my kitchen and I didn't feel like doing any more-so I didn't. However, the next day I was in the pantry and looking for peanuts and I couldn't find them. So I grabbed all the little containers of nuts and seeds that we had (big bags from Sam's, little packets for golf, and everything in between) and threw them into a giant box labeled NUTS AND SEEDS. A small part of me wanted to run to the store and buy matching bins to put everything into but then realistically I had to go to work, then coach, then my husband's basketball game soooooo Amazon box for the win!

5.   Use cardboard boxes and label things in your pantry

So, I already talked about this one above but you don't need to go buy fancy containers (you can do that later if it really bothers you).

Instead use what you have, see what sizes work for you, etc…It saves money and time.

6. Clean out car when get gas or go through car wash (always keep small trash bag inside car)

I started doing this on a day when they gave me a free cleansing cloth for the wash package I bought that day. So I wiped down my dash/cup holders/etc… while I was being pulled through the blinking soapy lights of the wash. When I finished, I threw the wipe on the floor of the passenger seat and realized that I had some other things that could be thrown away as well-receipts/a disposable coffee mug/etc… I also gathered up the spare change in my cup holders and put it into my purse for Paris (that is in the money section) When I exited the car wash, there was a trash can a few feet away. I didn't have time to vacuum and completely detail my car that day but the few tidying changes I made had the front seat of my car sparkling (the back seat is like a whole other country so don't ask about that!)

7. Slide clothes to other end of closet after you wear them

How does this tip help you? Well, it helps me to see what I have already worn and perhaps declutter anything that constantly sits in my closet and is unworn. Also if you are someone who doesn't like to repeat outfits, this is a simple way to remember what you have already worn.

8.   Use your stuff up before you buy more.

One of the biggest messes in my house (and I'm sure your house also) is having way too much stuff in the wrong places. Lots of magazines, shows, etc… try to convince you that if you would just organize it better, then you wouldn't have your current clutter problem. I am here to tell you that it is a lie. You have too much. Let's take bath soap as an example. Right now I have 4 types of shower gel and two different types of shampoo and conditioner (one for moisturizing and one for clarifying-ladies you understand). And yet, I was looking at buying a new bath gel because I really liked the scent. NOOOOOOO. So here is the deal I made with myself-I could buy the new bath gel after I used up 2 of the 4 bath soaps. And guess what? I still haven't gone through all that soap! So it is saving me time, money, and space to use up what I have first before buying new

I am currently using expired face lotion on my feet btw.

I am using my current hair oil before buying the new one I saw on Instagram

I am using my current face lotion before trying one that is sure to make me look younger.

9.   Have people over

This is one of the best cleaning tips. We moved into our new house and my husband announced to me that he had invited people over to watch football in 3 days. I was so mad at him! We had boxes everywhere! But then, with his help, we speedily unpacked and cleaned the bathrooms and kitchen. It was actually great (much more of a burst than a tiny tip) but it got my whole house unpacked in record time. I suggest having people over every couple of months. It forces you to pick things up, clean all the cobwebs in the corners and make sure things are painted/repaired/etc... Otherwise, life gets busy and sometimes when you know that no one is going to see your house, you get lazy with keeping it clean and orderly. It is the same with your car. Offer to drive your friends to dinner, colleagues to work, etc... It forces you to clean things up.

10.   Always carry something with you to another room

I saw this tip on the internet. So every time you leave a room, you take something with you that doesn't belong there. For example, your coffee cup doesn't belong in the living room-take it to the kitchen. Your hair tie doesn't belong in the basement, it belongs in the bathroom. Your dinner plate does not belong in the living room, it belongs in the kitchen. Getting items into their proper places is one step to getting things in order. This works great with kids. Make it a game! I am always amazed when people tell me that their teens have an entire kitchen's worth of utensils in their bedrooms. Reward them for every time they bring out a plate/fork/spoon/cup! Or better yet, don't let them eat in their rooms. By carrying something with you every time you leave the room, you aren't forced to spend an hour picking up the house. Things just naturally move toward their rightful place in your home.

11.   Declutter one/five/ten things a day

There are tons of Instagram and Pinterest posts about this one. Some people even post pictures of the things they are decluttering. The idea behind it is that you make a bit of a game out of it and each day you find something that doesn't need to be included in your life and at the end of 30 days, you are lighter. Your house is cleaner. I am currently working on this in my garage. Every time I go out there, I try to declutter something that shouldn't be there.

12.   Count number of seconds it takes and make it a game

I use this to clean the shower. I hate cleaning the shower. I think it is because I am 6'1 and bending over to scrub the floor is painful. However, my record is 118 seconds-I scrubbed fast! I keep a post it with the number 118 inside my bathroom cabinet and I try to beat 118 every time I clean! Start counting the minute you begin cleaning.

13.   Clear one surface

This tip is especially important for people who have a lot of stuff or clutter. Some of the spaces that people are trying to clean up are super overwhelming so they don't even start. Pick one small surface and clean that off (perhaps a coffee table). Do everything you can to keep that one surface clean. Even if it means dumping the stuff from the table in a different place. Keep one place clear and eventually your brain will enjoy it and want to have more stuff clear. I try to keep our dining table clear no matter what. I have found that the minute it gets cluttered, the whole kitchen looks like it is a mess. By keeping the table clear, other surfaces seem to stay clean as well.

14. One is enough

Henry David Thoreau said in his book Walden, "One is enough." I interpret this to mean that you only need ONE coffee mug. If you only use that one coffee mug, you will take very good care of it, wash it and never lose it. Think of it just like your phone. Most of us only have one so we take good care of it and rarely lose it. What if you only had one purse? Wouldn't you make sure that you had it with you all the time? Or one pen? One pair of sneakers? This tip is a nod to minimalism and deciding how much we really need in our lives. Less stuff equals less mess.

15. Don't waste valuable real estate for storage.

A lot of people put ALL their glasses in their kitchen cupboards. All their travel mugs. All their Tupperware. All their silverware. All their plates. All their kitchen towels and bowls and mugs. The reason that an Airbnb is so great is because the owner rarely puts in "too much stuff" unless they are getting it out of their own house. We rented one and it had 4 glasses, 4 plates, 4 forks, 4 coffee mugs, 4 wine glasses-you get the picture. There was TONS of space and it was a tiny lake house. They said in the listing that the house could sleep 4 so they provided enough for 4 and guess what? We had more than enough and if we used everything, there was a dishwasher. You don't have to store all your kitchen items in the kitchen, or all your clothes in your bedroom. Get some good containers and store things where you have room. Maybe your extra glasses go under the bed in the spare bedroom? Or your fine china is boxed up in the garage. One giant time waster is when your Tupperware falls out as you open the cabinet door. You curse as you pick it all back up and put it away. If you only had a couple in there, you would avoid this problem.

16. Keep cleaning supplies in the room they are used (and keep them out)

This is one of my greatest tips yet. I am fortunate to have two bathrooms in my house. However, I hated when I would "clean the bathrooms" and drip the toilet brush all the way through the hallway to clean the other bathroom. One day I went to the dollar store and bought a second brush to leave in the other bathroom-life changing! Also, I put another container of toilet cleaner in there. So every time I use that bathroom and it looks a little gross, the items are right there to clean it when I am done using it. I also keep a rag and glass cleaner/sink cleaner in each bathroom as well. Neither of them are full and I didn't buy brand new, I just used what I had and it is awesome! Now I don't have to worry about a cleaning bucket or hauling stuff through the house to clean. I also leave it out. It's just my husband and I-the kitchen cleaner is next to the sink. Stove cleaner next to the stove, toilet cleaner and brush next to the toilet. It reminds us to clean and if company comes over, I can shove everything under the sink in under 5 minutes for the entire house.

*Keep "under the sink" completely clear so that you can "shove" if company suddenly comes over.

17. Always have a Dopp kit packed

A Dopp kit is a travel kit for your toothpaste/shampoo/etc. When my dad got sick, I started keeping mine stocked at all times. It has a comb, shampoo, conditioner, soap, meds (I take one pill a day for prediabetes) Eyeliner, lipstick, mascara and some face lotion. Between that and 2 outfits I can stay anywhere for a week at a time (assuming that I have access to a washer and dryer for my clothes and underwear)

My ex-boyfriend was a traveling salesman and he always kept one packed. He also always kept his suitcase for work packed with underwear/socks/dress shoes so that all he had to do was grab his suits and shirts from the drycleaners and then pack them. He said he was very efficient at traveling and one time he was running late but still made his plane because everything was already packed.

18. Make piles

When I am cleaning and organizing, I make piles. It doesn't mean I always get to the piles right away but at least I can see what I have (I had a whole pile of travel tissue packs in my purse when I finally cleaned it out) and what I need to buy or don't need to buy.

19.   Have a dump room

Look, we all want a clean organized house where things magically get put away and it is never messy. However, my suggestion, if you have the room, is to have a dump room. Here's why. Yesterday I cleaned out a closet. I know what I wanted to fit into the closet and what I didn't. I didn't try to stuff it all back in. I put the other things in the dump room and I will decide at a different time if I want to organize them or get rid of them. Sometimes when I clean out my purse, I will have a dump bag that I put things I don't need into until I am ready to sort them. However, the kicker of this is that someday YOU HAVE TO ORGANIZE THE DUMP ROOM!!!!!! This is only a temporary solution. However, if you can keep 8 spaces clean and only 1 is messy, then I think it is a success.

20.   Buy sterilite drawers and have kids plan out Mon-Fri outfits

I saw this tip in a magazine. If you have young children, but the clear plastic sterilite drawers that come with 5 drawers. Then, on Sunday nights, help your kids to decide what they will wear all week. Socks, underwear, shirts, pants, shoes, coat-everything and stick it into a drawer that is labeled by day. This solves a few problems. 1. It saves time in the mornings. 2. You know as a parent what your kid is going to be wearing that week. 3. You can see if you need to wash anything.

21.   Reconsider where you store things

Cups go in the kitchen cabinets. Clothes go in the bedroom closet. Cleaning supplies go under the sink. If I walked into most American homes right now, no matter the size, they would be storing the above items in the same places as their neighbors. I am suggesting something different. My husband and I coach sports so we have a LOT of sweatpants, sweatshirts and workout gear. I tried for the last 10 years to organize those clothes in our closet with our other clothes. It would work for a few weeks and then everything would fall apart onto the floor.

Now I have stored all of our workout clothes in the hall closet. ALL of them! Shorts, t-shirts, sweatshirts, yoga pants, you name it, it is in there. Don't be afraid to look for alternative storage that works for you. Some of you may say, then where do you put your sheets and towels? Every bed has one extra set and I keep that in the bedroom, under the bed. The towels go under the sink because I have moved the cleaning supplies to sit out where they are used. (Tip 16)

22.   Dump clean laundry on bed

I read a lot of blogs of women that say the laundry sits in the dryer, in the laundry baskets, etc. after it is washed and dried. To prevent this, dump the clean laundry on your bed after it comes out of the dryer. It will force you to fold it and put it away so that you can go to sleep at night.

23.   Bra, underwear, sock drawer

I used to put all my bras, socks and underwear together in a drawer. I could never find what I was looking for so I bought nightstands that have 3 drawers in them. The first drawer is for bras, the second for underwear and the third for socks. (it is the order of which I put them on my body) and my husband does underwear, athletic socks, then dress socks in his 3 drawers. It is great. I always know where things are and they are easy to find when I am putting away laundry.

24.   Switch out seasons

If you don't have a big closet, you must use this next tip. Switch out your clothes for different seasons. Right now it is summer so my tank tops and shorts are in my closet. So are my golf clothes. I am not fighting with my winter sweaters right now. They are packed in a tote and will come out in a few months when it is time. I have some pieces of clothing that transcend the seasons (like shirts) and so those stay in my closet year round.

25.   Cleaning lady

If you have the means, get a cleaning woman. I don't care how tidy/clean/organized you are, it is the greatest feeling to come home from work and the house is completely cleaned and smelling great! Also (and I know a lot of people who agree with me on this) many people "clean before she comes" and make sure they tidy up so that all the person has to do is to actually clean and not put things away. This accountability keeps you from the mentality of "well it is just me living here so I can leave my clothes on the floor-they aren't hurting anyone" and forces you to stay on top of home maintenance.

26.   Move to right location (deodorant in bedroom)

So this is a bit of a weird one but it saves me frustration and a few seconds so I thought I would include it. After I shower, I wrap my towel around myself so that I can go to my bedroom and put my clothes on. I am too moist at that time to put deodorant on. But, I was putting on my clothes, heading back to the bathroom to finish getting ready and then forgetting to put on deodorant. So now my deodorant is on my nightstand. After my shower, I walk to my bedroom, put on bra and underwear and deodorant, put on the rest of my clothes, and then finish getting ready in the bathroom. This works for me. It would probably annoy other people-remember to do what works for you!

27.   Put at top or bottom of stairs

If you live in a two story house, put things that need to go upstairs at the bottom of the stairs and things that need to go downstairs at the top of the stairs. You may not have the energy or time to run things up and down but at least they are getting closer to their intended spot. When we buy groceries and laundry soap, I never carry the laundry soap down. It stays at the top of the stairs until I am making a trip down. That way, putting away groceries goes much faster.

28. Make a place for blankets/remotes

My sister has 3 kids, a husband and a dog. They all love to curl up in blankets at night when they are watching TV. However, when you go to her house, if the blankets are out, it looks messy because the blankets are everywhere! But her house is clean! My living room only has 3 blankets, but they make it look messy. So, now I have a basket for blankets and before we go to bed, they get thrown into it. Same with remote controls. There is a basket on the coffee table. Just those two baskets make the room look picked up and clean.

29. Hook instead of chair

I have lived in multiple bedrooms. I have noticed that when there is a chair or bench in the room, it tends to gather clothes/bags/shoes/laundry/etc…The way I have fixed this is to put a hook in my room. That hook holds my clothes for the next day (I set them out the night before) and then holds the hangers for me for when I return home from work and decide whether or not to rehang the clothes or put them in the dirty clothes. (teaching clothes don't always need to be washed every day. I teach high school so I don't get sweaty and the kids don't get me dirty). This one tip has kept my new bedroom clutter free. If you don't want hooks on your walls, put them on the back of your bathroom door or closet door.

30.   Day bin and night bin in bathroom

This has been a life changer. Bathrooms seem to always be a mess. For some reason, we feel as though we need EVERYTHING right at our fingertips. This creates a mess that has to be organized or put away every day. For the most part, there are certain things I use only in the morning (day cream, makeup, Hair brush, hair dryer, hairspray) and other things (contact solution that sits overnight, washcloths for face, floss, micellar water and cotton balls). So I got a bin that is big enough for EVERYTHING I use in the morning and another one for everything I use at night. I pull it out of the cupboard in the morning when I get ready, use everything and then put it back when I leave the bathroom. Same with the night bin. The only thing I leave out is my toothbrush and toothpaste because I use them at both times. NOTHING else is on my sink and it is always clean. It is awesome. It wasn't hard. It keeps me organized and in a pinch, I just throw it all in the bin quickly and shove it back into the cabinet. If you have multiple family members in the same bathroom, this will keep everyone's stuff separate and your sons won't be fighting with your daughter's makeup or straightener. Get them different color bins (maybe ones that match their toothbrushes and towel sets) then everyone will know what goes where.

31.   Washcloth to clean out sink at night

One way to keep the sink clean in the bathroom is to wash your face at night and then wipe down the sink and vanity with that wash cloth (assuming you don't use it the next day)

32. Towel not a bathmat

When you put your house on the market, a lot of realtors will tell you to pick up the bath mat so the bathroom looks more spacious. We did this for EVERY showing that we had and at one point I just threw it away. Instead, we used a towel and then after both our showers, I would throw our hand towels, wash cloths, bath towels and floor towel all into the washer and turn it on. (No one looks in the washer during a showing). When we got home we would throw everything in the dryer and be ready for the next day. That was a year ago and I have never gone back to a bathmat. Ever since I was little, I hated stepping on it when it was wet and it always felt "dirty". A towel prevents all of this because it can be washed easily with the towels. I currently use a turquoise or brown one for the floor and then white ones for our body so that we can differentiate. However, they all go to the wash together on wash day! It works great and then if there are any "water leaks" from the shower, I simply mop them up with this towel also.

33. Christmas mugs and clothes with Christmas decor

I have a few Christmas dishes and mugs. I used to keep them in the cupboards with my daily dishes but they all just seemed to get in the way. Now, I pack them up with my Christmas decor and get excited to see them when I pull everything out to decorate the day after Thanksgiving. It keeps my cupboards more organized and always surprises me when I see them after being packed up for 11 months.

34.   Pattern socks

When I started teaching, I realized that I would need "dress socks" and I HATE to fold socks. So I came up with my "Christmas sock" habit. If all of your socks are a pattern that only goes with one other sock, it makes laundry super easy! If you aren't super bold, you could buy Argyle patterned socks or polka dots.

35.   Separate laundry baskets for diff family members or colors

Laundry is an interesting concept. I learned that it goes like this. Wear the clothes. Put them in the hamper. When the hamper gets full, dump the hamper out and sort out colors. Then wash each load by color. Then dry. Then put everything into a laundry basket, bring it into the room, sort it all out and put it away. NO WONDER PEOPLE HATE LAUNDRY! Here's my tip if you have a lot of people in your family. Keep everyone's laundry separate. Wash THEIR laundry all at once and then give it back to them. Boom done. Most modern machines will work very well on cold water and dont need to separate colors (unless it is being washed the first time and it is red or dark denim). Plus, most people, especially kids, all wear the same type of clothes that can be washed together (jeans, t-shirts,sweats, etc...) If you have a professional job, you may need to wash things separately and hang them/iron them or have them dry cleaned. If you have a job like this, you probably already know which clothes have to be washed carefully.

36.   Don't fold socks

When I got married, I told my husband that I enjoyed doing laundry and would happily do his also but I did NOT "fold socks." I think he believed me to be joking. 14 years later, I still don't fold socks-his or mine and we have a bin in the bedroom where I put ALL loose socks, including my own. Sometimes he will spend some time sorting them and put them together. Other days he will simply go to the bin, pick 2 out and put them on. Doesn't matter to me but it REALLY speeds up laundry.

37.   1 load a day

A lot of people online subscribe to the "do a load of laundry every day." If that works for you, go for it. I feel that is a little too cumbersome. However, I don't have kids and we don't have a ton of laundry.

38.   Dishwasher every night before bed

This one is a must-even if it isn't totally full. It helps you to stay ahead of things. If you only have 2 coffee mugs in there, maybe don't run it but after a few dinners, run it. Tiny little steps are about maintenance so that things don't get overwhelming and lead us to have to spend an entire day to "unmuck" the house.

39. Little kids wash and dry and KEEP IN BASKETS (see tip 35).

If your kids are little and you are overwhelmed with trying to do their laundry, keep it in the basket. Then just grab it out of there when you get them dressed in the morning. Little ones can put their dirties in a hamper and get their clean clothes out of a basket. When they get a little older, they can help you put it away in drawers.

40. Lingerie bag for socks and undies

If you want to combine family members' laundry, invest in lingerie bags for each member. Then, all of their socks and underwear are together and you don't have to sort anything.

41. Sheet set-1 to wear and 1 while cleaning. Same with towel (Can always buy more) (unless special needs or baby) Also keep everyone same color or whole house same color (makes laundry easy)

Each bed in your house should have only 2 sets of sheets. Maybe 3 if you like flannel sheets for the winter. When you strip a bed, immediately put the clean sheets on so that if you can't get to that load during the day, you have somewhere to sleep at night.

Also, make the sheets and towels the same color for everyone or assign everyone a color. For example, you and your husband/partner have white sheets and white towels. Your daughter has yellow sheets and yellow towels. Your one son has blue sheets and towels and your other son has gray sheets and towels. Then, everything goes into the washer at the same time and each family member has clean sheets and towels. You can also assign each family member a day to wash. Your daughter gets it every Monday because she doesn't work or play sports on Monday. You and your husband get Sunday so that you can run the washer while he watches NFL football.

GET EXTRAS for babies or special needs children. When someone pees the bed, have a set that you can immediately put on so that you can wash the soiled items. My friend has a daughter with special needs who wets the bed every night. She has 7 sets of sheets for her bed in case laundry doesn't get done one day.

42. Unpack 1-2 things a day from the car/bag/backpack/moving box/etc...

If you have moved and need to unpack, just unpack one or two things a day. If it is something you don't want in your new life, put it in a pile to sell or donate.

43. Lazy Susan in cupboards and fridge.

Cupboards get messy. Especially when you have a lot of little bottles or containers. Use a lazy Susan to spin things around so they don't get knocked over or forgotten in the back.

44.   Keep backstock somewhere else

When I buy contact solution, they come in a two pack. I used to keep both bottles in the cupboard and I would knock over one to get to the other because I also had an extra shampoo bottle in there, and extra toothpaste, extra toilet paper, etc… Keep what you need and what you use daily close to you and then find somewhere else to store the extra. This will keep you uncluttered and save you time.

This applies to clothes as well. I kept stuffing ALL my workout shirts and shorts in a drawer and it would never close! Finally, I put 5 shirts and 5 shorts in there and put the "backstock" in a bin under my bed. I didn't get rid of them, I simply put them somewhere else so that when I put clothes away, everything fit and looked tidy. I did this with socks and scarves as well.

45.   Trash can every room

I went to a basketball game and the gymnasium had trash cans EVERYWHERE! Like an obsessive amount of trash cans. It seemed silly to me but I also noticed that it was one of the cleanest gymnasiums I had ever seen. And think about it, when the trash is full, people stop putting things in it or they set it nearby. If you have a trashcan in every room, trash can be thrown away easily instead of forgotten in one room and left there until someone goes back to that room. Also keep a trash sack in the car. Empty it after you go through the car wash (clean your car as you ride through the wash)

46.   Upstairs/downstairs vacuum

I am getting older and carrying a vacuum up and down the stairs is a struggle so when my vacuum was getting older, I bought a new one for the upstairs. Now I vacuum upstairs with the new one and downstairs with the old one. It makes it easier and quicker to have each one where it serves its purpose.

47.   Use dead time (Tv time at night to fold laundry/clean out purse/etc…)

TV time is a great time to do small tasks that you otherwise don't want to do-clean out purse, fold laundry, do dishes if you can see the TV from the kitchen, tidy up the living room, etc.)

48.   Make a chart of the outfits you can make with your current clothes (I have attached mine in the appendix).

It helps you to see what you already have and what you still need (I needed a navy skirt and a black skirt to make about 15 more outfits). It also helps you realize how much you have worn something and whether or not you should let it go or keep it. (I had a turquoise dress that I never would wear and so it was easy to let go of after looking at the chart.

49. Fold laundry (or some other mindless task) while you are on the phone.

Maybe you call your mom or sister every day. Is there something you could do while you talk to them? Laundry? Dust? Put away clothes? Some people call this "no extra time." You were going to make the phone call anyway so now you can get something done while you are also talking to a relative or friend. It's a win win.

50. Have zones for the things you don't like to do (socks)

Do socks REALLY need to be sorted and put away? Some would say yes. My sock bin would say no. They stay there until one of us feels like sorting socks or needing socks. Until then, they don't bother anyone and laundry is done super-fast.

51. Have a funeral outfit and an interview outfit

My father and grandmother passed away within 9 months of each other. My mother's best friend also passed away during that time. There are always so many emotions around death-finding an outfit that fits and shoes that work should not be on your mind. Same with an interview outfit. You don't want to try to interview for a promotion and search for pants that fit you the night before. You should be preparing your content! Check that you have these items (about once a year) and that they fit. If you have a spouse and/or kids, make sure they have one nice outfit also for weddings/funerals/school events/etc...

52. Separate clothes into zones for their function (golf, work, workout, etc.)

In my closet I have clothes separated by their function. In the summer, I have a golf clothes section. My closet isn't very big and so I do not allow those clothes to take up space the other 9 months of the year when I am not golfing. I have a plastic tote that I put them in when the summer is over. At that point I move some fall/winter workout clothes into that space in my closet.

53. One towel color for each family member

Buy every member of the family a separate color towel for the bathroom. If possible, match their sheets to it as well. Then when laundry happens, you wash it all together and give it back to each member. OR, make everyone's the same color so that all can go in the wash together.

54. One sock brand for each kid (Under Armor/Nike) or draw initial on toes

I saw this idea on social media. This mom bought all Nike socks for her one son. All Under Armor for her other son and then Champion brand for her third son. Then she never had to sort socks or wonder which kid they went to. I also know someone with 5 kids who wrote the first initial of each kid on the toe of the sock in Sharpie. VERY easy to sort when you're washing socks for 5 boys!

55.   Command center near door (pens/scissors/tape/)

It seems as though I always need to sign something or write a list right as I am walking out the door. I made a small command center right by the door so that I am not hunting for a pen/stamp/etc...as I am heading out the door.

56.   Color Code your closet

I hate searching for clothes. I have color coded my closet so that all my clothes are by their matching or same counterparts.

All my white/cream shirts are together. All my black shirts are together. All my tank tops are together. I have two green shirts and they are together. It just saves a bit of time when I am trying to put together an outfit. I.e. Black sweater, white shirt, skirt. Boom done. Pick one from each zone and move on.

57.   Toothpaste in the sink

Wipe it out each day. It keeps the sink remarkably clean and then you don't have to clean the bathroom as much.

58.   Clean before vacay

This one is magical. If you have the time, try to tidy up or clean before you go on vacation. Do the laundry, the dishes, make the beds, etc… When you get home, your house is nice and clean and you just feel better than coming back from a lovely vacation to a mess and all the junk you left.

59.   Keep "sometimes things" all in one spot-swimsuit bag

I keep my swimsuit, my husband's swimsuit, our two beach towels, sunscreen and beach blanket in my beach bag. It sits in the closet like this. It stays like this until we go to the beach. I keep all my tennis stuff in my tennis bag. School stuff in my school bag.

60.   Buy a baby crockpot

I have a mini crockpot that I use to take soup to school for lunch in the winter. I throw a can in my bag and off I go! It makes packing my lunch so much easier.

Chapter 7
Fall back (Failures)

No one likes to fail. No one likes to talk about it. Everyone wishes it didn't happen. However, it is a part of life. The difference is in how you use it.

If you fail at something and give up, then the failure wasn't useful.

If you fail at something and try again in a different way, then it was educational.

I think that all failure comes from trying something that was too hard or too far away from where we currently sit. Here is an example. Take two people. They both want to save $10,000 by the end of the summer. One of them has never saved a penny in his life. He has a low paying job and he doesn't even have a place to put the money like a savings account. The other person is used to saving, has a low paying job, and a savings account. He puts away $1.00 per day. Both people seem like they COULD save the $10,000 but the second person is going to have a way better shot at making it happen. He was closer to the end goal.

Here is another example. My friend runs 3-5 miles a day. I haven't run since my sophomore year in college. We could both make the goal to run a marathon but she has a way better chance of making it than I do. It isn't because of her ability. It is because she is closer to that end goal than I am. So, I will probably fail where she will succeed. We need to shorten the gap in order to succeed. If we both have the goal of putting on running shoes, we can both be successful. Then shorts. Then our earbuds. Then heading outside. Then walking to warm up. Then jogging ¼ mile, then ½ mile, etc…You get the picture.

So the question about failures then becomes, are you shooting too high? I am not telling you to never aim high. What I am telling you to realize is the gap between where you are and where you want to be is probably huge IF you are experiencing failure.

Now, I want you to figure out something you HAVE achieved. Is it because it was a goal that was slightly out of reach but not so far out of reach. Here is an example from my own life.

I wanted to write this book. I have wanted to write a book for years but it just seemed so overwhelming and hard so I would either write for a little bit and quit or not even try. Then I heard Gary Vee say "document everything" so that's what I started doing. Every day I would just write down a few things on a google doc-books I had read, experiments I had tried, etc… That was two years ago.

Finally, this summer I felt like I had enough material for a book (209 single spaced pages of notes) and so I started reviewing my notes and outlining. Here I am adding to the outline. Each little piece feels doable. My gap got smaller and smaller. Each time I get a little freaked out, I just go back to writing one little part of this book and here we are…85 pages later.

Another example from my own life comes from the teaching world. Picture a difficult student. This student struggles with relationships, studying, being on time, having materials, getting good grades, EVERYTHING. As a teacher, we see what the child can become. We see their capabilities and want them to reach for them. BUT, when a kid is super far away from what it actually takes to make their goals a reality, they get frustrated and quit or act out or pick on the student next to them. What the kid doesn't see (and sometimes adults don't either) is that the gap is too big-for right now.

I HATE when a D student says "I'm going to try really hard this year and get all A's". The gap is so large from where they are to where they want to be that they inevitably fail. Instead, we should be helping them with all the little tiny actions that will eventually get them to an A. Here are some examples. First, bring a writing utensil every day. Next, bring a notebook and folder (you would be amazed how tough this is for a lot of kids). Then, pay attention to the teacher for the first 10 minutes and last 10 minutes of class. (Remember-this is a student who is normally failing so we can't expect 60 minutes of rapt attention, 5 days a week. We have to build up to it) If a student can just do THOSE few things, in every class, their grades will naturally improve. Then a student can work up to not having any missing assignments (turn them in even if only one question is done), then not having any late assignments, then making sure every assignment is ¼ done, then ½ done, then ¾ done and then fully completed.

If you were a good student, you are laughing right now. These seem like simple tasks that should be easy to accomplish. However, I have been teaching middle and high school English for 18 years and have seen that these are NOT easy tasks and the ones I outlined above (if the student has never succeeded before) could take months or YEARS to get ironed out.

If a student got D's as a freshman, they should shoot for D+ C- as a sophomore, the C+ B- as a Junior and THEN try for A's and B's as a senior. Most kids and parents will NOT want to hear this. We live in a society of wanting (and getting-thanks Amazon) everything VERY quickly.

I haven't even touched homework, or studying, or going to bed on time, or organization, eating healthy food (Not giant caffeinated drinks) or learning disabilities. There are so many little pieces that go into being a good student and getting good grades and so many kids see what they want (good grades) and have no idea of all the little things it takes to get there. They see their friends that have good grades, think they are doing the same things as them, and when they don't accomplish the same grades, they assume they are "dumb" and give up.

There was a great Cosby show episode that detailed this perfectly. The niece had come to live with the family and she would have her friends over to study. They would eat pizza, dance, and study a little bit. She couldn't understand why her friend got A's on the tests and she got D's. Her friend then told her that the "studying they did" together was just fun time hanging out and then she would go home and put in some actual study time. She assumed that her friend did the same (she did not) and thus the life lesson of the episode.

So if you have a goal that you are failing at, take a look at how far you are from it.

Are you trying to lose 30 pounds but you have never even lost 1 pound before?

Are you trying to wake up an hour early to get things done but you have never been an early riser?

Are you trying to save money but you don't even have a savings account?

Are you trying to get a promotion at work but you can't even really handle your current job?

Think of yourself as a struggling student. Keep your goals and dreams high but start putting your effort into MUCH smaller actions.

Try these small actions instead.

Are you trying to lose 30 pounds but you have never even lost 1 pound before? (give up your after dinner ice cream one night a week)

Are you trying to wake up an hour early to get things done but you have never been an early riser? (wake up 1 minute earlier each day so that you get up 5 minutes earlier by Friday)

Are you trying to save money but you don't even have a savings account? (start collecting spare change around your house/car/purse and put it in a jar)

Are you trying to get a promotion at work but you can't even really handle your current job? (Show up 15 minutes early or stay 15 minutes later and put in a little extra work on a certain project)

In summary, you need to use failure to teach you, not to force you to give up. Go smaller and smaller and smaller until you are successful. Then once you have been successful, you can increase the tiny actions in the positive direction.

Chapter 8
Bursts

So this chapter is a bit different from the others. This chapter will have an entire mini book dedicated to it (by next year) but I want to lay down some of the logistics. A "burst" is when you make a LOT of progress toward your goal very quickly. Examples include Whole 30, A spending fast, cutting out sugar for a certain time period, exercising a lot more, deep cleaning your house, etc…

So let's say you are tiny stepping your way to increasing your physical shape. You are taking tiny little steps each day to get more steps in and you are averaging about 7000 steps a day. Then one Saturday morning, you wake up and decide to take a walk. Then you come home and feel great so you clean out the garage. Then you shower and get dressed and run errands and when you finally crash that night, you see that you have gotten 12000 steps. And it feels GOOD! You think to yourself "I can do 12000 steps every day!" Then the next day comes and life returns to normal and you only get 7200 steps and you feel disappointed and defeated and frustrated.

You have experienced a BURST.

The biggest hiccup is thinking that this is your new level. USUALLY it is not.

Your body was ready for the 12000 steps that one day but not for 12000 steps EVERY day. It was a burst. Call it what it was (planned or unplanned) and go back to regularly scheduled programming.

The key is to recognize when it is a burst and when it isn't. Also be aware of when the burst is ending and DO NOT get mad at yourself. Here is an example from this summer.

So today 8/10/22 was a burst day. I had a cup of coffee, started writing and put some laundry in. Then I washed the cat's bedding. Then moved some furniture to the basement and set up the new cat litter down there. Then cleaned up the kitchen and swept under the rug. Then vacuumed. Then cleaned my bathroom. Then did another load of laundry and towels. Then decluttered a few things. Then wrote some more and listened to a podcast. I was JUST starting to sort out things in my closet and a wave of fatigue hit me. The burst was over. For whatever reason, I am tired. It is 2 pm and I am tired.

I am guessing that it is partly due to the fact that my body shuts down around this time. In the summer I can nap. During the school day I push forward to the end of the day and go home. On the one hand, I see a ton of stuff that I still want to get done **but this is the key to using the burst**. I have learned that when it is over it is over and to not beat myself up over it but instead to be happy with what I did accomplish.

In conjunction with the tiny actions, I have been throwing in a few 30 day burst challenges. These are TOUGH. Do not attempt them until you have mastered the tiny challenges or you really want to challenge yourself.

I am currently in the middle of 30 days of no potato chips and it is going great. I eat nuts if I am looking for a salty treat and the few times I have been in a restaurant, I order cottage cheese. It turns out you can't really eat a ton of cottage cheese the same way you can a ton of potato chips. My husband does this and will go entire months where he is "French Fry Free."

I am also on day 17 of no social media. This experiment/burst is going amazing! I have read 8 books, finally worked on my own book and gotten a ton accomplished around the house.

In previous years I have done a No Spend November and No Sugar month. All of these have gone quite well, so I am excited to write more about them. They are NOT the tiny incremental method. They are a complete abstinence from a certain habit. Remember Chapter 1 about minding the gap and knowing where you are? I am ready for these challenges because I have been playing around with the tiny habits for years. You PROBABLY are not ready to go cold turkey on some of these topics and THAT IS OK! You can build up to them if you want to, or not. It's up to you! You can still be successful toward your goals if you don't use the burst/abstinence method. Some ideas include:

30 days no spend

30 days no sugar

30 days no sitting (more steps)

30 days no scrolling/social media

30 days no stress

30 days no swearing

30 days no self-doubt

30 days no carbs

30 days of no time wasting at work

However, it has been my experience that these "bursts" can get you to your goal quicker. Just keep that in mind if you are under a time crunch to accomplish something. You could also try a mini burst. (one week or ½ the month)

Update! So today 8/23/22 and yesterday are EXACTLY what I am talking about with a burst and exactly what I want to show you MIGHT happen (it happened to me all the time before realizing how to more efficiently achieve my goals-tiny actions!)

So I played pickleball yesterday (well, hit the ball around) and after 30 minutes, I was POOPED! My husband called to ask how it went and I immediately said "am I in that bad of shape?" Now being the loving husband that he is (but also a basketball coach at heart) he replied with "well you haven't really moved around that much this summer." I scoffed at him! He must be kidding. I was SOOOOO active this summer! I didn't feel like I had hardly any downtime.

So I checked my Fitbit for the week/month/3 month and year averages…Well… I averaged about 7000 steps this summer-not bad but not really "active" and then I looked at my step average when I was teaching…also 7000. Hmmmm… I know that a step count isn't the be all end all of fitness but when I was thinner (about 2 years ago) I was averaging 10000-12000 a day and sometimes more. Even if NOTHING else changed…5000 steps is a lot of extra movement and it would explain why I feel like I can't lose weight. So I did what so many of us do. I declared that I would "get in better shape!" and I hit 12000 steps yesterday and 11000 today. So I thought to myself, well this is easy. However, I go back to school tomorrow and any teacher can tell you that "reentry is hard!" so I am going to TINY step my way toward 10000 steps again instead of jumping right in and starting a new teaching job as well as trying to up my steps. (Which would normally result in failure in about a month)

I will shoot for 8000 average in September 2022, 9000 in October 2022 and 10000 in November 2022. I will increase by about 250 steps a week. I may hit the goal sooner and if I do-AWESOME! But if I don't, this is a very doable plan. I do NOT want to get burned out in the first month and quit (that is what this whole book is trying to prevent).

Other bursts I am taking part in right now are the no sugar challenge. The no social media challenge and the no potato chip challenge. So far so good! A few mishaps here and there but overall I am doing fantastically!

And on Day 4, I STRUGGLED to hit 8000 steps so I got to 8000 and went to bed! I felt accomplished!

Chapter 9
Day in the Life

So what does this really look like in practice?

Here is a typical day

5:45 Alarm rings. Stumble to shower. Shower. Put floor towel on edge of tub to dry. Walk in a towel back to my room. Put on underwear, bra, deodorant. Grab outfit from off hook. Put hangers back on hook. Head to bathroom to finish getting ready. Take out the "morning box" that has only my essential morning things in it to get ready (makeup/hair dryer). When finished, put that whole basket back into my cupboard. Hang up my towel, put bath towel for feet on edge of tub, brush teeth. Use washcloth or hand to clean out sink. Leave restroom.

6:30 start making coffee while I pack my lunch. Same lunch every day. Cheese sticks, pack of nuts, Atkins bar and a salad. Put ice in my water bottle and start coffee brewing. I either empty the dishwasher or wash hand wash only dishes in sink while coffee brews.

6:40 Grab my school back which was packed the night before with laptop, school papers, extra pens, snack, deodorant, grab my car keys off a hook by the door and head to my car. (Back of car has a gym bag in it with full set of clothes and workout shoes in case I am somewhere waiting and could walk a few minutes)

7:00 am arrive at school. Desk is clean from night before. I take a few graded papers out of my bag, sign into my email, check my plans for the day and make second cup of coffee. Kids do not arrive until 7:45. I DO NOT wander the halls looking for people. I use that 45 minutes like my life depends upon it-doing all the things I don't want to have to do later (make copies, reply to emails, grade quizzes, etc...)

8-3:30 School (at lunch I wash out my lunch dishes and coffee travel mug so that I don't have to do it at home) Desk is cleaned off and plans for the next day are sitting out.

Drive home by 4. Grab ONE ITEM from the garage and either put it in its proper place or get rid of it. (We moved last year and still have boxes in the garage)

Clean out my school bag and lunch bag. Put dishes where they should be so I can pack in the morning. Repack everything for the next day that doesn't need to be refrigerated (set coffee mug by maker, etc...)

4:15-5. Walk outside or on a treadmill. May put in a load of laundry before I head out the door.

5-6:30-ish prep/cook dinner and then put all dishes in the dishwasher or hand wash them and RUN IT.

6:30 Take out the "night box" Wash face, brush your teeth and put it back in the cabinet. Put on pjs and lay out clothes for the next day. If we are just watching TV, I might do another load of laundry, sort some socks, put away paid bills (I keep them all for 2 years just in case)

9:30 go to bed. When I remove comforter, I put it right in front of closet door/hook with my outfit for the next day on it so that I HAVE to throw it back on the bed in order to get to clothes.

Some of the unseen things you might miss. Grocery shop on Sunday mornings. Take my stinky socks downstairs with me and bring up a glass that someone left downstairs last night. Sorted mail as soon as I got home (bills to pay go on fridge, important papers to keep go in my office in a basket (until tax time) magazines or cards go in a pile to be read and recycled.

So if you do all that Monday through Friday, you don't need a big cleaning day on the weekend. I might vacuum the living room. I sweep the kitchen floor when my coffee is brewing or dinner is cooking. I clean the toilets during one of the times that I use them at night. I dust during commercials.

I will be truthful that I don't have kids and I try to keep a lot of junk out of the house so that it doesn't get cluttered.

My days are maintenance. Notice I did not talk about cleaning out the garage or decluttering the storage room or even decluttering my office. Each day I will do a little more until it is done. I REFUSE to spend a precious weekend on cleaning! We recently had a party to watch football and the whole house (upstairs and downstairs) took about 30 minutes to clean. Everything was already picked up and mostly put away so we dusted, ran the vacuum, scrubbed the guest toilet and boom! It was done!

Chapter 10
Where do I go from here?

I have only a few goals for you and this book

1. You were able to read this book quickly

2. You thought of a few things that you could add to your life that would make it easier.

3. You saw where you may have gone wrong in the past.

4. You now have a plan for how to move forward in the future.

If you think these tiny actions don't matter, just know that I stopped doing them and my house got dirty quickly. My desk at work was a mess. My clothes were all over the place. I was forgetting things to take to school. These tiny actions matter.

If you want to check out my blog at www.tallgirltinyhabits.com I provide weekly updates as to how things are going for me.

Additional books to read and resources I highly recommend are below. The appendix contains a clothing chart I mentioned and also "rough notes" from my No Spend November. You can look forward to a whole book on bursts by next year!

Thanks for reading!

Jessica

Resources

These books are amazing and you should check them out!

Atomic Habits by James Clear

Mini Habits by Stephen Guise

Tiny Habits by BJ Fogg

Hello Habits by Fumio Sasaki

The 1 percent rule by Tommy Baker

The Compound Effect by Darren Hardy

The Power of Habit by Charles Duhigg

Project 333 by Courtney Carver

The More of Less by Joshua Becker

Grit by Angela Duckworkth

Appendix

No spend November notes

These are ROUGH notes but if you are intrigued, feel free to sort through them for the good stuff!

These are not edited-they are from my journal during my very first No spend November

I also gave up candy that month.

Day 1 Update

Well...I didn't eat any candy so that is awesome. And I ALMOST didn't spend any money. My husband is a basketball coach and he needed to buy an app and his wallet was in the car. It was 900 at night and raining out. I was not going to make him run all the way down there to get it-even though I secretly wanted to so that I could officially not spend any money yesterday. He said he would give me the 10 dollars so that I technically didn't spend money. And I accepted!

Day 2. Baseball scrimmage tonight so will need to get food on the road and might need gas but food and gas are acceptable purchases. However, I will try to keep them to a minimum. I am also trying no mayonnaise November. And I need to get some fish oil capsules. I have a blood test in 5 weeks and I need my cholesterol to be lower. Got Culvers-10 bucks! Man that's really expensive!

Day 3

Had to get gas this morning 32.00. Then I spent 6 dollars for Crockpot Friday at school. My husband gave me back the 10 dollars from the app I bought. Also, we scouted a baseball game so we ate on the road. Subway had a buy one get one deal so 2 sandwiches chips and a drink was only 10 dollars. Awesome! Then, I used 2 dollars at the game to buy cookies and support a family who was struggling. It's not hard to not buy when you are so busy! I haven't watched TV in 3 days and I won't really have time next week either so that helps. However, there is a Christmas display at work and since I have separate Christmas money, I am going to purchase these books for 14.00. It will be for 2 of my nieces and they are sticker books so I know they are a good deal!

Also, taking a yeti to school from now on because I have already purchased the communal water for the year, but I don't drink it every day so going to start doing that!

Day 4

Away baseball game. Got a lot of grading done in the morning. Then rode to the school with Brian. A parent had provided dinner for us. Then 10 hours of baseball. After, I need a smoothie to keep me awake as I drove the hour home alone. I bought a small and when they asked to donate a dollar to the Ronald Mc Donald House, I said sure! Then ai immediately regretted it. It's no spend November! I was so mad! It only took 4 days to break my resolve. It wasn't food or drink! How could I?

Then I had to relax, give myself a break...after all I didn't buy a pair of pants! And that leads to me today....

Day 5

I CAN NOT find my favorite pair of black pants. The pants that i wear almost every week for work. They are comfortable and look good and they are nowhere to be found. I'm so upset. So what would I normally do. Get online and buy a few pair of pants, have them shipped to my house and try them on, send back the ones I don't like. Now here's where no spend November comes in and I AM sticking to this. I have 2 pairs of black pants. They are not as comfy ad the ones that are lost, but I do have some I can wear. They will be fine. I will be fine. This is why I am doing this. I have many other pairs of pants in many colors. I have skirts and dresses. I still have clothes in my closet that I haven't worn yet this school year. I am extremely blessed. I'm not happy about it and through my sorting, I found an entire bag of clothes I can give away/sell. I saw a post on Facebook 5hat said. You eat out 10 bucks a day for lunch. 10 times 30 is 300. 3 months is 900 dollars. You have money to travel but you hate making sandwiches. I laughed out loud! So true!

Day 6.

Darn it! Yesterday I needed contact solution, soap and feminine hygiene products Now. I didn't buy anything extra so that is awesome and I used some reward points I have so it cost 42 dollars but it still made me mad. And they WERE things I needed. I'm almost out of contact solution and soap and girl stuff. I am also proud that I have been offered candy and I have refused. It has been a huge step in the right direction so that's good :)

Day 7. Holy crap-almost bought a car! What is wrong with me?!?!??! It was going to be a 650-dollar payment for 39 months!!!!!!!! JESSICA! Use your head! Yes, you could afford it. But is that really what you want your money going to?????

This started because the Stabilitrak light came on Sunday and it shuddered at a stoplight. Problem is, I am under water on it-not sure how that happened and so car dealers would have to roll my current payoff into a new payment. PLUS, I had to put 2000 down AND I WAS OK WITH IT!!!!!!!!!!!!!!! Thankfully husband talked me off the ledge and I told the dealership...no. in an email this morning. I should really calculate exactly how long it takes me to make 650 dollars.

On a positive note-am drinking the water at school (remembered my YETI). Didn't stop and grab fast food on way home-made pasta instead. Brought pasta for tonight in case food here isn't good. So should be another NO SPEND day. It is currently Nov 8. I write these the next day. Kind of recap what happened the day before.

Do we buy stuff so that we feel good enough? What if just being me was good enough? Stripped down of all the stuff...am I good enough? Good enough for what? For breathing? For love? For a job? For friends? For myself? Would a new car make me a better person? I might feel like a more successful person in it...But...what does that really mean? What is success? Who is success for? Is it so you get up in the morning and work hard at your job? I'm getting very philosophical.

If you can't do the little things well, you will never do the big things well. What are the little things?

The no spend November is helping me see the little bits of money that we waste each day. A dollar here, ten dollars there. How much of a difference would that make in our lives?

Could you retire sooner? Live simpler? What is at the root of our buying and wanting? Is it comfort? Ease? Security? I want all of those things but buying a new pair of boots isn't going to give them to me. However, telling myself I'm enough in this world might

I want to look good, feel good, feel important, feel worthy. So we spend money to make people like us, love us and respect us. Who are the people I respect the most? My granny and she is more frugal than anyone else in our family and I love her for that. I see friends and family wasting money on stuff and I wonder if it makes them happy? Why buy a big house? Why buy a new car? However, fixing the old one is getting annoying but for 650 a month I can GO TO MAUI! THATS AMAZING! I want to go to Vegas for New years and for 2 moths of that added payment, my husband and I can go. So... what are my priorities really?

There are SO MANY SALES! And so many emails, commercials, trying to sell me stuff! I don't need more stuff. This no spend thing has been good. I would love to save a ton of money at the end of it. I wonder if I could continue it through December? What if that money could make it so we can go to Vegas?

Day 10 (Nov 10)

So it's the end of week 1-pretty much and it looks like I have saved about 90 bucks. I'm kind of disappointed it isn't more. However, I do have 90 in cash that I haven't spent so that's good and I haven't had to dip into my savings of 200 a week toward paying off car so that's good too. It's expensive to live that's what sucks. All I have bought is necessities and food and gas and I still spent 110 in the last 10 days. Today I am spending 6 dollars for crockpot. I ate the school provided food during conferences and ate at home instead of eating out. My goal right now is to pay off CC each week. And keep the savings for somewhere? But where? Should I keep it in my travel account or hair and clothes account? I don't know…

It is kind of amazing all the times that money trickles out of your pocket and you just aren't aware. Also, people ask you to buy things all the time and it is nice to say 'No Spend November" and just move on

The article I read yesterday is that I need to increase my savings. I think I'm pretty good right now with retirement savings but I guess I can pay off car and then save more? I have 20 more days and I hope I can stay this strong. If I save 90 a week then I can have 400 a month which then I can put toward paying off car or in my corvette fund…

THAT is important to me. I really want a convertible

If I can stick with this, it means that I can save almost 1200 a month right now (on top of HSA, IRA and 403b) and by God I better be doing that! Think of how that will set me up for my future!

Even if we were to buy a house, I could keep saving like this. Maybe not as much but a good chunk.

Day 13. Nov 13.

It is SOOOOOOOOOOOOOOOO excited to think of how much money I'm saving. It is really an astounding amount. I'm wondering if I could sustain this for a whole year? Or half a year? I'm not sure but it is super exciting to think that I am almost half way done with the month and I don't really have a desire to buy anything. I think the "no repeat clothing" thing is showing me how much I really have in the world. Also, the fact that I brought some new clothes and makeup right before this also helps.

The longer I go, the easier it is becoming. I wonder if I can set big savings goals like 50000 or paying off car or paying for vacay

Day 15.

Half way through No-spend November and I really think I can do this long term. I keep thinking of Gary Vee and how he says that if you can suffer for 2 years, you can live like a king the rest of your life. Could that really be true? Could I really not spend any money or very little for an entire year? Could I pay off so many debts that it made it worth it? Really my only debt is my car but if that was totally paid off I would have an ADDITIONAL 400 a month to spend or save. That could be amazing! Not to mention all this other money that I could save. That could be amazing too. Car needed oil change and engine debunker. So, got to pay for that. Just paid for gas 25 and gas on Monday was 10 dollars

Day 16

I really want to buy a book. I have run through my SSR books and I want a new one. It would only be 3 dollars on my kindle but as you can probably imagine, the minute I cave in, then I feel like the whole experiment was a waste. It wasn't implemented to see how little I could spend; it was implemented to stop wasteful spending. Many would argue that I book isn't wasteful spending. However, it is not a necessity and in

14 days I could buy it. One thought I have been having is that EVERYTHING I own was a want at one time. And now, I WANT something different. So what if I change my wants? What if I borrow and utilize what I have instead of buying? Could I really hold myself to only spending a small amount on my wants each month? What would that number be? And would it stretch from 100 to 150 to 200? When you say No Spend November, it becomes very clear.

Day 20.

Feel like I'm getting ready to crash and burn. I had to buy cat food and litter 50 bucks. We went out to eat Sat. 45 bucks. I have to pick up the sweatshirt I custom ordered back in October 60 bucks. This week I feel like I won't save anything and will even dip into savings from last week which will make me very sad. However, I have been setting aside 800 a month to pay off car early and I WONT have to dip into that, so that's good! However, I think I got a little cocky last week thinking I could do this forever. But maybe every other month? December is going to be hard. I already committed to helping one of my homeless students get some clothes and donating to the cookie party for him as well. While I am not spending the money on myself which is good, I am still spending the money...and it makes me feel badly…

Ok. got to focus here. It's not as dire as it seems. I have REALLY cut back on spending so that is good! And I'm trying to increase savings and pay off debt. Albeit however slowly. Also, I have to pay for a hotel in Cleveland for my appointment. Also need to pay for background check for PH. Just made Christmas budget and also ordered an Amazon gift card that I can use to pay for some of the gifts for the nieces.

Proud of myself. Just went to dollar store and didn't buy cute Christmas things.

Need to give away Cute Christmas things...want to make Buckeye balls and give them away. I think that would be fun

Day 22.

Didn't spend today except for gas yesterday. Bought a pop and chips at school. Had massive headache. Had to.

Day24

Today was black Friday. I only bought the 3 amazon Christmas gifts that were in my car and decreased in price. They were 50 dollars and I have Christmas money set aside for that. Also ordered Christmas cards because they were half off. Again, using set aside Christmas money for that. 20 dollars. I wanted to buy hand soaps for the office that were half off today. However, I am resisting. I wanted the all bean sweaters in the catalog that were also half off but again I resisted. As I took a shower today, I realized an interesting mindset with purchasing things. "I have a good job, I have the money, I am not in debt except for car, I put away money for retirement, I wear second hand clothes, I deserve it and I can afford it". But...just because I can afford it, does that mean I should buy it? THAT is a much bigger question. What does affordability truly mean? That I have the money in my pocket or bank account so I can afford it. Or is affordability just a made up term. Is it only if you can buy it outright that you can afford it? If that's true, then none of us can afford our houses or our cars our lifestyles. should we all wait a good chunk of our lives to afford our dream house? We looked at a $200,000.00 house on

Wednesday. So much money for nothing. How much money will I truly save with this no spend November? I reimbursed myself for the union dues and the oil change so I'm trying to put everything else on cc to see what I spend. In December, I really want to continue it but I feel like I need to buy stuff. Could I do a pause and think before I buy it?

Day 25

Shattered phone

Day 26

Bought new iPhone for 900 dollars :(

Day 27.

Ok so here is the interesting part. Since I had to buy the phone, I figured well forget it and just buy the kindle book and the temple spa stuff because of cyber Monday but no no no no.

I realized that I have an all or nothing mentality and that I need to shake that off.

Get back on the horse-got 4 more days. Just because it is on sale does not mean I need it

Also, found my black pants. Yippee

Also been able to get some gift cards with points so don't have to spend as much on Christmas gifts so that's fun and exciting. Kind of want to make/give a gift to people at school and kind of don't. I want to make buckeye balls and also want a gift for baseball girls.

Look at the stuff that I really don't want as bad now

Day 28.

I bought pizza last night from Little Caesars and it was disgusting. I threw mine away and have had a stomach ache all day :(I am so tired also don't really want to be here so glad I learned how to type without looking at keyboard I wonder if there is a place I could see how many words per minute I can type. I can type 44. That's awesome. So much better than 13 when I was in high school. hahahaha

Day 30

Saved about 800 for the month (on top of IRA/403b/HSA)

The capsule wardrobe chart for school

I own all of these things with the exception of the black and navy skirt (bought them)

If I wear each outfit 3 times I should make it through the whole school year. On Fridays we wear a school shirt and jeans so I did not include those. These are outfits I made from the clothes I already owned.

At the end of the year, I will sell/give away anything I didn't use. This is kind of a capsule wardrobe but it isn't the minimalist version that Courtney Carver uses in her Project 333.

			Black blazer black shirt khaki skirt
			Black blazer black shirt khaki pants
			Black blazer white shirt khaki skirt
			Black blazer white shirt khaki pants
			Black blazer black shirt gray skirt
			Black blazer black shirt gray pants
			Black blazer white shirt gray skirt
			Black blazer white shirt gray pants
			Navy sweater white shirt khaki skirt
			Navy sweater white shirt khaki pants
			Navy sweater white shirt gray skirt
			Navy sweater white shirt gray pants
			Gray sweater black shirt black pants
			Gray sweater black shirt black skirt
			Gray sweater white shirt black pants
			Gray sweater white shirt black skirt
			Gray sweater white shirt navy pants
			Gray sweater white shirt navy skirt
			Gray sweater white shirt gray skirt

				Brown sweater/blazer white shirt black pant
				Brown sweater/blazer white shirt khaki pant
				Brown sweater/blazer white shirt black skirt
				Brown sweater/blazer white shirt khaki skirt
				Brown sweater/blazer black shirt black pant
				Brown sweater/blazer black shirt black skirt
				Green blazer black shirt black pants
				Green blazer black shirt black skirt
				Green blazer white shirt black pants
				Green blazer white shirt black skirt
				Green blazer white shirt navy pants
				Green blazer white shirt navy skirt
				Purple blazer black shirt black pants
				Purple blazer black shirt black skirt
				Purple blazer white shirt black pants
				Purple blazer black shirt black skirt
				Purple blazer white shirt gray pants
				Purple blazer white shirt gray skirt

			Maroon blazer black shirt black pants
			Maroon blazer white shirt navy pants
			Maroon blazer white shirt black pants
			Maroon blazer white shirt navy skirt
			Maroon blazer white shirt black skirt
			Maroon blazer white shirt khaki pants
			Maroon blazer white shirt khaki skirt
			Maroon blazer white shirt gray pants
			Maroon blazer white shirt gray skirt
			Black dress gray sweater
			Black dress purple blazer
			Black dress brown sweater
			Black dress maroon blazer
			Black dress green blazer

14 One offs

				Black and white striped dress
				Black white and red striped dress
				Green and Navy Dress
				Purple Dress
				Red and black skirt
				Gray leaves skirt
				Black and white skirts (2)
				Pink skirt
				Gray checked pants
				Red checked pants
				Maroon checked pants
				Pink sweater
				Black and white sweater
				Navy striped sweater
				Yellow skirt (maybe not)
				Pink and black dress (maybe not)
				Turquoise dress (probably not)
				Leopard shirt
				Green sweater set (Probably Not)
				Black and white striped long sleeve
				Denim shirt
				Cranberry blazer and striped shirt
				Black lace skirt
				Blue long sleeve
				Pink long sleeve